W9-BTH-552

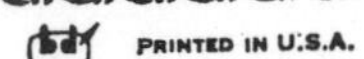
PRINTED IN U.S.A.

33-26

171

A LAYMAN'S GUIDE TO PRESBYTERIAN BELIEFS

A LAYMAN'S GUIDE TO PRESBYTERIAN BELIEFS

by
ADDISON H. LEITCH

ADDED FEATURE:
An Analysis of the Confession of 1967

ZONDERVAN PUBLISHING HOUSE
GRAND RAPIDS, MICHIGAN

A Layman's Guide to Presbyterian Beliefs

First Edition
Printed in the U.S.A.
Library of Congress Catalog Card No.: 67-11617

INTRODUCTION

Generally it is difficult for one who has grown up in one denomination to distinguish or even remember the divisions in another denomination, and I suppose this must be true of those who wonder about the various divisions among Presbyterians. We have in the United States the United Presbyterian Church in the United States of America and the next largest body, the Presbyterian Church in the United States. In a popular sense these are generally known as Northern Presbyterians and Southern Presbyterians, the division having taken place at the time of the Civil War. In Canada some of the Presbyterians have joined the United Church and there still is an on-going Presbyterian Church, and in the United States there have been several divisions over a wide variety of differences giving rise to Orthodox Presbyterians, the Faith Presbyterians, the Cumberland Presbyterians and the like. Some have said that we can speak of the P's, the U.P.'s, and the split P's. It is difficult then to say what it is we mean by Presbyterian beliefs if we are to pursue the issues which led to these divisions.

The question of Presbyterian beliefs is made even more difficult in our day by the fact that the United Presbyterian Church (the Northern Church) is now engaged in writing and debating a new confession which is to be known as "The Confession of 1967." It is impossible at the present writing to say what this particular branch of Presbyterianism will be presenting to the world as its confessional stance, but we expect to know by May of 1967.

In writing, therefore, on the subject of Presbyterian beliefs one must decide at the outset what constitutes the major body of belief common to all these groups and keeping in mind also the background of a "new" confession. Presbyterians in the large have continued to think of themselves as related in some way to the Westminster Confession. There are those who hold to the whole confession in every detail. But the larger churches have been speaking in recent years of only the "*system* of doctrine" of the Westminster Confession, and now with the "New Confession of 1967" there may well be some clear departures from even the *system* of doctrine of the Westminster Confession. We are on safe ground, however, if we follow the general teachings of the Wesminster Confession recognizing that in the next few years some Presbyterians in particular and perhaps Presbyterians in general may be shifting away from this basic document. The Westminster Confession is too large a document to be carefully analyzed in a work of this sort, and we must recognize also that much of what is in the Wesminster Confession is common to all Christians and not necessarily distinctive Presbyterian doctrine.

In sum, therefore, it will be our attempt to speak of Presbyterian beliefs as those beliefs related to the Westminster Confession common to all the Presbyterian denominations and to treat these doctrines in such fashion as to bring out what makes them Presbyterian as against what they might be if held by some other denomination. Almost any other writer coming up to the same task would perhaps choose different doctrines for analysis or choose different ways for emphasizing the same doctrines in giving *A Layman's Guide to Presbyterian Beliefs.*

CONTENTS

A LAYMAN'S GUIDE TO PRESBYTERIAN BELIEFS

Chapter One

THE HOLY SCRIPTURES

INTRODUCTION

In company with all Protestants the Presbyterians have held to the special authority of the Holy Scriptures. We all recognize what can be called general revelation or natural revelation. Even the Bible itself allows for this. "The heavens declare the glory of God." Or again "there is a light that lights every man coming into the world," and as Paul states it, "eternal power and Godhead are clearly seen through the things that are made." Indeed one of the arguments of the existence of God is simply an observation of the world of nature giving rise to the natural question as to what has brought the marvelous world into being, some first cause accounting for all the wonderful things which surround us. The Roman Catholics also have recognized "natural revelation" and have, indeed, given considerable study to "Natural Law."

At the same time there are many great questions which nature does not answer, and many great truths which we could not learn by simply observing the natural world itself. We need a clue to suffering, for example. We have great questions as to beginnings and endings, and purposes, and whether "the whole show" makes any sense at all. We wonder whether there is something desperately wrong with man which makes so many of his grand schemes end in ashes, and at the same time we wonder if there is any saving strength apart from man which can save him from his morass. Sometimes the world seems utterly beautiful and our hearts are filled with "intimations of immortality," but the world can be terribly ugly, full of cruelty and injustice and vice. Men can rise to heights of loyalty and courage or sink in their perversions beneath the level of self-respecting animals.

It has been a common belief among Christians that God has given us *special* revelation in the Holy Scriptures. Just as we can know many true things *about* our friends, we can never really know our friends beyond their willingness to reveal their inner natures to us. All persons, like all things, are in some sense hidden unless they make their own revelation. It has been held by Protestants generally, therefore, that God has revealed Himself in the Scriptures, and that apart from the Scriptures we cannot know about eternal purpose or the hope for immortality or the victory of good over evil. The nature of God is revealed in the Trinity. We learn the true nature of sin and the answer to sin in the plan of salvation. Unless God had been willing to reveal these truths to us we would never have been able to learn them from nature, and when He did reveal them to us, He had to reveal them in some authoritative fashion, and this authoritative record is the Word written. This is not to deny, as we shall shortly discover, the living Word in Jesus Christ. But we could not even know about Christ, what it was He came to do, or what it was He really said, apart from the written record. To quote something which I have written on a former occasion, "With all kinds of things seen somewhat, and half-seen, and variously fused and diffused in depth and focus and color, we put on 'the divine spectacles' (John Calvin's figure for the Scriptures) to see clearly in proper perspective what we are aware of in general but could not quite make out."

The eminent Divines who drew up the Westminster Confession, therefore, put at the very outset of their confession their chapter titled "Of the Holy Scriptures" and made it very clear that what was to follow in the Westminster Confession would come directly from Scripture itself, or be necessarily implied from Scripture. They recognized, as we have already suggested, "that the light of nature in the works of creation and providence" are revealing of the nature of God, but they also recognized that this natural revelation was not sufficient for our salvation, that it pleased God to give us the special revelation of the Scriptures, for which reason we must consider Holy Scripture "to be most necessary." It is almost impossible to emphasize enough how basic the Scriptures are to the understanding of the Westminster Confession. No departure from the Scriptures is permitted. The body of truth contained in the Scriptures is complete and nothing else is necessary.

From this foundation they continue to write of Scripture, setting forth the sixty-six books of the Bible all of which they insist are given by inspiration of God, and they further make clear that these sixty-six books of the Old and New Testaments which are listed in the Confession itself are to be distinguished from the apocryphal writings which have their own worth as religious essays, but which are not to be considered as authoritative. We are to pay attention to the Bible because it is from God and not from man.

We know that it was in this period of history that men were anxious to put the Scriptures in the common speech of men everywhere. This was the work of Wycliffe in England. This was the reason for Luther's great effort in producing the German Bible in the vernacular. The Westminster Divines pursued this same idea in insisting in their chapter on the Scriptures that the record of the Bible is clear enough for the learned and the unlearned and should be translated for people everywhere. Although the Bible is not a simple book, even though at its heart it has a simple message, we are not to be led into believing that it can be understood only by scholars. It can be understood sufficiently by the common man to serve him as a guide and support him in his Christian life. Where things are difficult to understand we are to take it as a basic rule that the Scriptures themselves are the best interpreter of Scripture, and that a man who studies the whole Gospel of God can without special scholarship in such things as archaeology, history, or language come to a sufficient understanding of Scripture through Scripture itself.

The Westminster Confession

One distinctive on the Scriptures appears in the fifth point in the fifth division in the great section on the Scriptures in the Westminster Confession. They sum up for us the arguments a man might use to support the Bible as from God, and perhaps our best approach is to quote what they have to say.

> We may be moved and induced by the testimony of the church to an high and relevant esteem of the Holy Scriptures, and the heavenlies of the matter, the efficacy of the doctrine, the majesty of the style, the consent of all the parts, the scope of the whole, (which is to give all glory to God), the full discovery it makes of the only way of man's salvation, the many other incomparable excellencies, and the entire perfection thereof, are arguments by which it does abundantly evidence itself to be the Word of God; yet, not withstanding, our sure persuasion and assurance of the infallible truth, and divine authority thereof, is the work of the Holy Spirit, bearing witness by and with the Word in our hearts.

This is a tremendous statement and needs to be looked at carefully because in our day it represents a center for controversy regarding the way in which the Church is to use the Bible.

See what is said. In the first place there are many *reasons* why a man ought to believe that the Bible comes from God – the matter, the efficacy, the majesty, the agreement of all the parts, the scope, the plan of salvation, and "many other incomparable excellencies." These arguments for the Bible as a unique document have been used for centuries and were brought to very sharp point in the writings of Calvin and are given this particular form in the Westminster Confession. Following Calvin's origin, the Westminster Divines assure us, however, that these so-called "rational purposes" are not sufficient, and that there must be the inner testimony of the Holy Spirit. It is difficult, indeed impossible, to prove to a non-believer by reasons alone that the Bible is the Word of God. It is equally impossible to take away from a believer his assurance that the Bible is, indeed, the Word of

God. We are dealing here with a view of Scripture which has dominated the Presbyterian structure from the time of Calvin to the present day.

Presbyterians do not hold to any worship of the words themselves (Bibliolatry). They do not hold alone "to the letter that killeth" but insist at the same time on "the spirit that maketh alive." On the other hand they will not let go of the written record and accept only the freedom of the spirit. Theirs is not a religion of the "inner light." It is Presbyterian belief that a sound doctrine of Scripture is the inner-locking and interlocking of the Word and the Spirit: the control and discipline of the written record given wings by the work of the spirit. This is how we believe that Christians can be led into all truth. We do not get any new revelation above and beyond that already written, but we do need the enlightenment of the Spirit of God, the spirit of truth, to discover from the written record, not the guide and light of the men of Bible times, but the guide and light for our own day.

For example, it took men 1,900 years to discover what had to be done about slavery, but this was not a new revelation. It was simply the work of the Spirit of God on the revelation already writen. By the same token we can reasonably expect that the Bible can tell us, under the guidance of the Spirit, the answers we so desperately need for the problems of race, war, or poverty or any other pressing problem. The Spirit of God that gave us the Bible by inspiration will be the same Spirit that uses the Bible that He gave us to tell us what some passage means for modern times. To put it in other words, the Bible as written is "the only infallible rule of faith and practice," but this is never to be thought of apart from the work of the Spirit playing upon the written Word. We read "in the spirit." We preach under the guidance of the Spirit. We discover what we are to do because it is the work of the Spirit to "take of the things of Christ and show them unto us." This is how the Spirit is to lead us into all truth, not because there is to be new truth apart from the Scriptures, but rather a new understanding of what the Scriptures already say. The reformed doctrine of the Scriptures is

Word-Spirit or, if you wish, Spirit-Word; the two are never to be separate.

The Debate in Presbyterianism

Within the Presbyterian Church today there is considerable debate at this very point. Under the influence and impact of the great theologian, Karl Barth, men have been led to see that there is a sense in which the Word of God begins with the written record, continues through the reading and preaching of that record, is received by the reader or the hearer, and is finally applied in the act of response. Karl Barth thinks of the Word as that total process by which God through the written record speaks His word to men in the situation in which men now find themselves. It is possible, therefore, for different men to find different ways of guidance from the same written document. The words of Scripture become the channel or the vehicle through which the Word comes alive finally in the life of the believer himself. There is great truth in this, and the emphasis needs to be made. Believers themselves are finally to be "epistles known and read of all men." The Word which comes through the words of Scripture becomes in some fashion a living Word in us. The church as the body of Christ, expresses the life of Christ whereby the church is truly at work.

No one could or should deny this process. The only area of debate is whether the Holy Spirit of God now gives us *new* truth in our living situations in our modern times instead of the truth once and for all delivered. Insofar as Presbyterians hold to the Westminster Confession they must hold to the fact that "it stands written," and our expectancy is that the Spirit of God on the basis of what was delivered "once and for all" interprets for us meanings and guides us finally into action. The whole Bible, the whole council of God, is effective in this fashion, and believers expect it to be so; no new truth, but new light on the Truth.

Some modern critics such as Bultmann (and their approach is not really new) pick and choose certain portions of Scripture as authoritative while eliminating other parts as being irrelevant in our culture and in our modern climate and atmosphere of opinion. The Westminster Confession cannot allow this. There is a "canon" of Scripture which includes all sixty-six books, and "all scripture is inspired of God." When we talk about Word-Spirit, we are talking about the Spirit of God using the whole body of written documents. If certain parts of the Bible seem irrelevant to our own day, it may be that we may need those very parts as a judgment on our day. Our particular culture is not the judge of the Scriptures but the Scriptures are the judge of our culture. It is not so much a question of the way things *are* as it is a question of the way things *ought to be.* We may grant that certain portions of Scripture are more relevant at different times than at others and this particular day in which we live may need certain guide lines, for example, more than in mediaeval times; by the same token our day may be under peculiar judgments not needed in other times. But no man and no group of men is capable of saying that any part of the Canon is irrelevant; and, therefore, pick and choose according to his own tastes.

There are certain Christian groups, notably the Roman Catholics, who would equate human tradition with the written record of Scripture. Presbyterian doctrine in the light of Westminster cannot condone this. The guide for the church as for the individual is the authority of the Scriptures. Churches in council may pray for and expect guidance of the spirit but only on the basis of the written record. This would prevent, for example, the Roman Church discovering and maintaining such a doctrine as the infallibility of the Pope or the Assumption of Mary. If they look upon the church as having authority equal to the Scriptures, it follows that the church may present these new doctrines. But this sort of thinking is not acceptable in the Reformed tradition. In terms of Westminster again what the church confesses must rather come from the Scriptures or be necessarily implied from what the Scripture teaches, and anything above and beyond this is of man and not of God. It is true that the Scriptures are not entirely of "private interpretation," and we need the study and control of the whole church over against our own private enlightenment. But even here in the last analysis a man's assurance of truth is "from inward work of the Holy Spirit bearing witness by and with the word in our hearts."

CHAPTER 1 – *Questions for Discussion*

1. What is meant by natural revelation? Give some examples.
2. What sorts of questions are not answered by natural revelation?
3. Why do Presbyterians insist on both the Word and the Spirit?
4. What is the relationship between the words of the Bible and Christ the Living Word?
5. What contribution did Karl Barth make to the use of the Scriptures?
6. How does Bultmann use Scripture?
7. How do the Roman Catholics use Scripture and tradition?

Chapter Two

THE SOVEREIGNTY OF GOD

It is J. B. Phillips in our day who has written a book entitled *Your God Is Too Small.* Apart from the way in which Phillips himself treats this subject, I think we can agree that many of the questions which plague us regarding our most holy faith arise with this fact; namely, that our thinking about God makes Him too small.

This is true in spite of the fact that on Sunday morning in practically every church service, Christians repeat the Apostles' Creed, saying, "I believe in God the Father Almighty, maker of heaven and earth." What this means is a little harder to conceive of than we think when we say the words of the Apostles' Creed so glibly. It would be a good exercise sometime to try to think steadily about the idea of "God Almighty," and then to think of Him as "maker of heaven and earth."

Our telescopes continue to reach out into what now appears to us to be boundless space. Although we can hardly conceive of the idea of infinity, our astronomers are showing us increasingly that space is boundless, that it is infinite. Even to talk about space at all is to talk about something that goes on and on beyond the powers of our mind to grasp. In order to deal with space we have to break it up into bits and pieces like miles or yards or inches which we can handle.

At the other end are microscopes which focus or project us from what we are able actually to see to lead us into infinitesimal bits of matter. We go down and down into molecules and atoms and electrons and mesons, and the end is not yet. Rightly considered, the molecules themselves seem to be little universes. As Pascal pointed out long ago, "Man seems to stand halfway between the unseen infinites of space and the infinites of matter." Man, who thinks about these grand matters, is a mystery to himself, not only when he tries to consider what man is as mankind, but when the tries to plumb the mysteries of his own personal being.

The Nature of God

When we speak of "God Almighty, maker of heaven and earth," we are talking about the Creator and the sustainer of all that we know and the infinite reaches of possibility that we do not know. It is possible, also, to think of God as being so almighty that the whole universe from its outer reaches to its inner bits and pieces may well be as small in relationship to God as molecules themselves are in relationship to man. It could be that God does indeed hold all things "in the hollow of His hand," and that what seems so puzzling from our viewpoint is no more puzzling to Him than a grain of sand which we hold in our own hand. These infinite things are for God the "small dust in the balance" and the nations from such a viewpoint are as "a drop in the bucket."

The more we think along these lines the more we realize how superficial our thinking can be when we rattle off something about "Almighty God." At the same time this kind of thinking about God is, perhaps, the one and only clue to many of our questions. Things that seem impossible from our viewpoint on the face of it ought not to be so impossible to One who holds all things in His hands, who sees the end from the beginning ("our times are in thy hand," Psalm 31:15), and who has available to Himself every possible combination of solutions to every possible combination of problems. One would not expect that things which are puzzling to us would necessarily be puzzling to that kind of a God, and one should not be anxious, as we so frequently are, that to that kind of a God anything really ever gets out of hand. For a Christian there is added to his belief the idea that this Almighty God is a God of infinite wisdom, and if one may believe the revelation in Christ, a God of infinite and constant self-giving love. Whatever the final answers, if one's faith is big enough, he may assume that God Almighty is in charge, and that the God who is in charge is like Jesus Christ. One can trust such a God, and the supreme exercise of faith is to believe that "underneath are the everlasting arms." The only alternative is the absolute abyss. It may well be in our day that the general loss of faith in God among men is the basic reason for the utter despair and the sense of absurdity which mark what we call the "beat generation."

To think of God in terms of almightiness, however, has constantly raised many of the same kinds of questions in the minds of thinking men and women. If God is as great as we say, how can He be concerned with problems as small as ours are? This idea rocked the church at the time of Copernicus when it became clearly evident that the earth is not even the center of the solar system let alone of the galaxy of which it is a part (although it is a nice question what we mean by "center" in a universe which has no bounds – any point could be a center). As men came to a sense of the vastness of the universe, they reacted immediately with the question of how anything as small as the earth, or even worse, as small as the men who inhabit the earth, could be of any importance in a universe so vast, or to the God who controlled such a universe. With our modern telescopes and microscopes, the question which faced the church in the day of Copernicus is magnified many times.

Perhaps here, too, we ought to rethink our thinking. Does not this kind of question grow out of the false view that something is of value according to its size? We know better than this, and all kinds of illustrations lie readily at hand. It is childish thinking to believe that a nickel is worth more than a dime because it is bigger, that a chunk of coal is worth more than a diamond, or that the oyster shell is worth more than the pearl. On more personal levels what can you say about the baby in the household? Is it not true in a love relationship (and Jesus keeps insisting that the relationship is a love relationship) that it is a mark of most homes that the baby of the household, the weakest member and the one farthest from fulfillment, is the one who receives the greatest care and on whom infinite value is placed? Would we love a baby more if it were born six feet tall? Would the son of the household be worth more if he weighed a ton? The asking of such ridiculous questions gives its own automatic answers. The questions make no sense because they have no relationship to reality. Why do we ask the same kind of question with regard to the importance of a small planet in a large universe? And, if we do, we ought to reassess our questions.

The Administrator

Another line of thinking that is helpful is to think again about what marks the administration of any man we know who is really in charge. Is such a man careless about little things? Is it not rather true that the mark of a good administrator is that he is much concerned about little things knowing full well how the little things affect the big things? This is one of the reasons, I suppose, why so many leaders in industry have worked their way up through the company. They know how everything functions, and where everything ought to be. Carelessness about little things in such a man we consider inexcusable. If you have been employed by such a man, was it not always a constant surprise to you how everything eventually crossed his desk? Was it not even a part of your admiration of him to recognize how he had "*everything* under control"?

Some years ago I was on the coaching staff of a college in Pennsylvania, and sat in on the meetings where salesmen tried to convince us of the merits of their goods. On one occasion we were buying new basketball uniforms, and the salesman kept insisting that we ought to buy long colored socks rather than short white ones. "Long socks will increase the speed of your team 25 per cent," the salesman insisted, and of course that was something greatly to be desired. I am not sure, beyond his enthusiasm to sell his product, that long socks will increase the speed of a basketball team 25 per cent, but I certainly do understand his point. If you have ever watched a high-speed collegiate basketball game, you are frequently impressed by the amazing quickness with which a highly-trained basketball player can see what he has to do and do it. Sometimes good players seem to have eyes in the backs of their heads. When the crowd is going wild, because someone is moving up behind the player to steal the ball from him, at the very last second the player seems to see the danger and flick the ball away. As the whole team moves down the floor on a fast break, all the man with the ball sees is a flick of color out of the corner of his eye and this is enough to dictate his next move. It is only because he has this kind of vision and senses these almost infinitesimal differences that a star player is able to move so amazingly fast and with such grace and decision. These little things have to be a part of his total consciousness all the time.

One night I was driving home in a blinding snowstorm and even when I dimmed my lights to get rid of the reflection of the snowflakes it seemed to me that I was closed in by a wall of flickering white. Thousands and thousands, and I suppose millions, of snowflakes were falling all about me, and by the next morning the minute little bodies would become a major task for the snowplows. The little things were beginning to make a big difference. More to the point, however, was the knowledge I had gained somewhere, that in some marvelous fashion each of these countless snowflakes had the same basic design — they were snowflakes not something else — and each one in turn had its own individual design. Think of the meticulous care of the Creator in the constancy of structure and the beauty of design.

We all have our favorite trees somewhere around the yard or somewhere around the community. This one is a maple, that one is an oak, and how do we distinguish them? Well, among other things, we distinguish them by the shape of their leaves. It is not hard to tell the difference between an oak leaf and a maple leaf. There is a basic design in each case. At the same time botanists assure us that each individual leaf is different from every other leaf in spite of their likeness in kind or species.

And what shall we say of people? It has been the custom in recent years for people to send out clever announcements when a new baby arrives. The one we like best came from a college friend. She had written the notes in her own hand, and each note to her friends had this one message. "John has arrived and said, 'Move over. I'm here.'" How true. One of the delights of the birth of a child is that he has appeared as a normal human being. We are always glad because he looks human and belongs to the human family. But the deeper delight is this: someone new has really arrived; no one like him before or ever again, and we certainly are not wrong in thinking there is something special about our own child. There is. What kind of a world is it, or better yet, what kind of a power is in control of a world like this, where such things come to pass?

Cause and Effect

There is yet another kind of wonder here. It is the wonder of relationships. Not only do we find outstanding designs in individual things, but we find that everything is related to everything else in the universe in some kind of cause-effect relationship. Nothing just happens in and of itself. There are causes and effects, and when we see effects we automatically and naturally look for causes.

Some years ago in the *Reader's Digest* there was an account of two people who were sitting in their living room on about the eleventh floor of a large apartment building. They had the window open to allow the breezes to blow, and were suddenly startled to see a man drop on the window sill. He plunged through the open window, dashed for the door, and ran down the hall. The man of the house sprang to his feet and was after him immediately but never caught him. He and his wife could not discover that night nor in the days afterward where the stranger had come from, and they could find out from no one in the apartments above where he had started his strange and startling trip. For days the man could not get this problem out of his mind, and then one day his wife brightly suggested to him, "Never mind. Some things just happen." But she was wrong. Things never "just happen," and the man was right in insisting on discovering some kind of cause and effect relationship.

If a purple cow should appear at your doorway while you are reading this, you would say immediately, "Somebody *must* have painted the cow." Notice that word *must*. Or you might argue that you are drunk or having some kind of hallucination. Purple cows don't just happen. There must be some reason for their appearance.

Such simple illustrations in no way minimize the profound truth: it is the nature of our minds to believe that all things are interrelated. Again we see things don't just happen.

Predestination

Presbyterians have often been jokingly described as those who believe in predestination. In fact, this is the first thing people generally think about a Presbyterian, "He is the kind of person who believes in that strange doctrine of predestination." Does a Presbyterian mean to say that we have no such thing as free will? Does he mean to say that our experience of free choice is playing us false?

What we need to understand is that the whole idea of predestination among Presbyterians, in the Reformed tradition and among Calvinists, is an attempt to express religiously what certainly appears in the Bible record; but at the same time is giving expression to a problem which is not only a religious problem but one of the deepest problems in human thought. For the moment we can think about it apart from its religious meanings. Basically it is this question of cause and effect; nothing "just happens."

Let us suppose that one of our modern juvenile delinquents has been brought before a judge. The law stands and the judge must judge according to the law. But he will want also to judge according to equity, and in such a judgment he will give some weight to the facts of the boy's heredity and of the boy's environment. In *some sense,* whatever free and responsible choice the young man has made and for which he is to be judged as a criminal, his choice already is conditioned by things over which he had no control even while making his free choice. It is one of the great problems of our age to determine and weigh the extent to which a person is to be blamed for what he does. The sins of a whole society make for the sins of a person in that society. As Reinhold Niebuhr has suggested, the moral man in the immoral society cannot make an absolute moral choice because everything he does is conditioned by what life has in some sense made out of him as well as the ambiguous situation in which he is forced to make his choice.

In sociology and psychology, as well as in jurisprudence, we have become increasingly aware that great forces in our culture have so conditioned us that a so-called free choice is free only in one who is already in some sense led to his choice. Before a youngster is two years of age, where he might make what is called a moral choice, he has already been conditioned by his family and their circumstances – the pictures on the walls of his home, the music in the air, the conversations and anxieties reflected at the dinner table, the weight given by his particular family to such things as money or ambition or honesty or decency. If we say he makes a free choice in his adult years, we have to remember that the man who makes the choice is the man who has been shaped in some sense by circumstances which he did not freely choose.

The other side of this problem is what we mean when we talk about a thing called character. If you were to tell me of a certain friend of mine who had done a dishonest act, I would have to answer, "He couldn't do a thing like that." Do I mean to say that he is not free to act dishonestly? As a matter of fact, I glory in the fact that a man of his character (fixity if you like) *cannot* do such a dishonest act. If I am going to argue whether he is free to do such a thing, I have to look again at what I mean by the word "free." In some sense he is free (theoretically), but in some sense he is not free (actually). How is it that we can say that we "count on" our friends? If certain laws of nature don't always work the same way, and if certain people have not somewhere determined a fixity of character in which their friends can rest, we can't count on anything. We are all, of course, finite creatures subject to error and to sin, and we cannot insist that an honest person can *never* be dishonest, but we could hardly carry on a day's work if there weren't enough people around whose words were as good as their bonds. People are the way they are, and this is one of the expectancies of our being able to move through life at all. They can do wrong, and we can be wrong in our judgment of them; but in the large we are recognizing that by the time of maturity a person is what he is and this is the sort of thing one would always expect of him.

What is true of individuals is certainly true of cultures, and sociologists are increasingly impressed in our day by the grip that our cultural relationships have on everything we do. If we may fall back again on what was said previously, no one fact nor factor of reality is unrelated. Therefore, we cannot say that what a man is can possibly be unrelated to everything that has come into his makeup.

Man's Freedom

We must never speak of this fixity in such an extreme fashion, however, that we do not allow at the same time for its opposite, a man's freedom. This is a paradox from which we cannot possibly escape. To return to our illustration of the juvenile delinquent. If the judge goes so far as to say that the boy cannot possibly be to blame for what has has done, he takes away from that boy the most precious thing he has; namely, his personal right finally to make up his own mind. The law understands this, and that is why a man is responsible for his crime (and in making him responsible we are really doing him a favor), and the only way we can relieve him of this responsibility is to relieve him of the best he has by insisting that he was drunk or insane or for the time being not *himself*. Men have struggled with this problem for hundreds of years: to what extent is a man bound and to what extent is a man free? The answer is not clear or final, but at least we must see the magnitude of the question, and we must not blame religion. We can hardly blame the Calvinists when they say, (1) Destiny is built into a man, and (2) A man is always responsible for his own moral acts. How these two apparent opposites can be put together is another question, part of the mystery of the way things are, but we cannot deny that both sides of the question exist, and we are superficial if we try to dismiss either side of the question.

The Bible itself is clear on both sides of this issue. "No man cometh unto me except the Father draw him," and at the same time, "Whosoever will, let him come," or again, "Work out your own salvation with fear and trembling for it is God who worketh in you." At the same time that the Bible insists that God initiates, sustains, and controls all things (and He cannot control the big things unless He controls the little things—"Not a sparrow falls without the Father") the Bible also insists that a man shall keep the commandments and that he shall be judged on the last great day in the light of what he has chosen to do.

We are not ready to speak of God's eternal decrees (this will come in a later chapter), but this is a good place to note what the Westminster Divines did with this moot question. Watch how they swing from one side to the other of what is a problem, not only of religion, but of every area of profound thought. "God from all eternity did by the most wise and holy counsel of his own will, freely and unchangeably ordain whatsoever comes to pass." This is clear enough. Everything, that is *everything*, is of God's will. But read on. "Yet so as neither is God the author of sin nor is violence offered to the will of the creatures, nor is the liberty of second causes taken away."

It is a strange and wonderful doctrine, but even if the Bible did not suggest it, it would still be with us. One of my all-time favorite baseball players was Stan Musial of the St. Louis Cardinals, "Stan the Man." My own home was in Pittsburgh, Pennsylvania, and Stan Musial's home was in a small town near Pittsburgh. I am sure that during his whole career the Pittsburgh Pirates would have given almost any amount of money to have this "local boy" on the Pittsburgh team. They couldn't buy, and St. Louis wouldn't sell. Why? The men involved in such a transaction would have been and were indeed hardheaded businessmen interested in the business of baseball as well as in the pleasure of the game. Why did Stan Musial mean so much money? Basically because businessmen and sportsmen knew that he would bat .300 or better during the next season. How could they know such a thing? Did anyone or anything make Musial bat .300? And yet season after season he did. This was his great value.

In spite of all this there was nothing automatic about what he did. In any given baseball season he was faced with multitudes of free choices. Every time he was up at bat he had to decide on each pitch. Meanwhile the catcher was making his choice of signals, the pitcher was accepting or refusing the signals. The infielders and outfielders shifted to meet the threat of the batter, the coach on the bench was signaling his word to various members of the defensive team, and another ball was finally thrown. Stan would swing or he would not swing. And this happened in game after game day after day. At the end of the season his batting average again was over .300. Was he fixed or free? And the amazing thing about it was that he seemed to enjoy every minute of it!

The Bible says, "In His will is our peace," or again, "Ye shall know the truth, and the truth shall make you free." As you see, the Word of God is a revelation of truth in spite of the fact that men can come at much of the truth from other directions. And the truth is that God is absolutely supreme, which means that He is in control of all things. If not a sparrow falls without the Father can we believe that any man is born into the kingdom without Him, and *at that same time* a man is responsible for his choice; yet in some way his responsibility for his choice is bound up in the sweep of God's will. It is no accident that a man like Calvin, who is insistent on the absolute supremacy of God, is at the same time one of our great writers on the subject of prayer. Does not Calvin think man's prayer life mechanical or automatic? Does he mean that prayers are just exercises with no real issues at stake, or does not he mean, as the Bible surely insists that "prayer changes things" even while he talks about the immutable and unchangeable will of God? There is a mystery here when we try to resolve it on merely an academic level. But when we think about it in terms of living experience, we discover that both God's sovereign action and our responsible action can be true, and that we live comfortably within such a structure.

One of the most interesting truths about the sovereignty of God is that historically it has always been looked upon as a doctrine of strength. Since it is rooted and grounded in a personal God and has to do with relationships with a personal God, it cannot be either fatalism or determinism and has never been so considered in the Calvinistic tradition. Men like Paul and Augustine and Calvin were profound thinkers and were strong believers in God's absolute sovereignty; and they were strong, very strong, individuals and moved to change things about them. "It is no longer I that live but Christ that liveth in me," said Paul. Or again, "For me to live is Christ," and yet Paul was most himself when he was most obedient to the will of God. He had his greatest personal fulfillment when he obeyed. Jonathan Edwards, who probably had the greatest mind America ever produced, insisted that his mind was "subservient" to the mind of Christ. And yet how creative he was – and free! Free to change his manner of living, free to change life around him, free, indeed, to create a whole era in American history.

If we may take Calvin as an example (and he is usually "blamed" for the Presbyterian characteristic doctrine of predestination or the over-emphasis on the absolute sovereignty of God), we can see how this doctrine was for him a doctrine of strength. Geneva was a beleaguered city and the people in Geneva were under the pressure of the king and the pope. The king could take away a man's life. The pope could determine a man's eternal destiny. But Calvin convinced his followers that they were in the hands of God utterly and completely and could, therefore, stand up to king and pope. This became the "iron" of Calvinism which we see in the Beggars of Holland, the Puritans of England, and the Covenanters of Scotland. These who should have been so bound by God's almightiness were free men, and their lives became a foundation for everything we know of freedom. A man who could stand in the presence of God would not have to bow down to king or pope. We must remind ourselves that this iron of Calvinism worked its way into the beliefs of the Baptists and the Episcopalians and is in no way foreign to the thinking of Luther and all the churches that bear his name.

Contrasting Philosophies

Perhaps the fact that the Wesleyan movement seemed to throw its emphasis on the side of moral freedom as against God's sovereignty may also have its historical reasons. Unthinking people can easily condemn the Calvinistic emphasis on the absolute sovereignty of God as leading to fatalism – the Kismet of Islam – and this kind of lightweight thinking was abroad in the day of Wesley. The Wesley brothers, both products of the Episcopal Church with the Thirty-Nine Articles which reflected true Calvinism, faced a different kind of problem in cleaning up the cesspools of Great Britain. How easy it was to find a drunk in the ditch who could excuse himself by saying, "Well, here I am, but it is the will of God." Wesley had to insist on the other side of the truth, "Stand on your feet. Be a man." In a like situation today either side of this question can be emphasized: the control of God or the responsibility of man. All things are of God. He initiates, sustains, and carries through according to His purpose. But to quote the Westminster divines again, "But not so as to do violence . . . to the will of the creatures nor is the liberty or contingency of second causes taken away."

It was my privilege some years ago to do my doctor's degree on the subject *The Relevance of Calvin to Issues Within Modern Protestantism.* My supervisor was Dr. John Whale of Cambridge University, who was then considered the leading authority on Calvin in the English language. Time and again he said to me, "Our civilization needs Calvinism! We need to understand what he was really saying." Why do we need it? It can be a doctrine of strength in anxious days. The Almighty God, the maker of heaven and earth, is in control of all things.

At the same time some interpretations of Calvinism, as well as much that has come in modern psychology, has been tempting us to say that man is nothing but a tool in the hands of the forces of determinism or in the sweep of history and is, therefore, not to be blamed for what he does. A kind of moral irresponsibility is abroad in our times. This true Calvinism faces. It is the belief of Presbyterians that God is "absolute," but that with this sovereignty man is required to make moral decisions for God's sake.

CHAPTER 2 – *Questions for Discussion*

1. Criticize your own view of the term "God Almighty."
2. How do you put the almightiness of God together with His wisdom and His love?
3. Does "God Almighty" make it difficult to believe that He cares about little things? Explain.
4. How is our thinking about God corrected by our recognition of the relationships and designs of the universe?
5. Does our constant appeal to the laws of the universe say something about the nature of God?
6. What is meant by the term predestination?
7. Is predestination only a religious problem?
8. How is predestination related to moral freedom?
9. Can a person be free who is also bound?
10. Explain predestination as a doctrine which gives strength to Calvinism.

Chapter Three

THE SIN OF MAN AND FREEDOM

One of the most impressive qualities about the Scriptures is the fact that one may return to them again and again and discover depths of meaning which had before somehow evaded him. We discover in the reading of ordinary literature that normally we have quickly plumbed the depths of the message and the messenger, and it is a rare book that will bring us back to a second or third reading. The Bible, however, has been the kind of book that men have returned to a countless number of times. Even though the message is frequently apparent on the surface, that same message can become the heart and center of a man's lifetime of study. Always there appears to be fresh insights.

This is clearly illustrated in the opening chapters of Genesis. In chapter one we read about the creation of the world. In chapter two we read about the creation of man, and in chapter three we read about the beginning of sin. A superficial reading of these three chapters can give the impression that it is pretty simple stuff and in one sense it is. The language is neither scientific nor philosophical; all of it reads like a story, and it is the kind of story that one can read to children with the expectancy that they will get the gist of it. But we must not be betrayed by this apparent simplicity. It has the same kind of simplicity (not simple-mindedness) of the atmosphere around us which is, indeed, simple stuff. However, it is an atmosphere one can analyze into space, the gases in space, or the suspension of liquids in space, or the ability of this space to carry radio or television or radar. In other words, it is the kind of space one can move through and look through. This is the kind of simplicity one gets when he sees the blue of the sky as he looks through space into infinite distance.

So it is with these opening chapters. The simple story has to be told so that simple minds can grasp it, yet there is always much more than meets the eye. The first chapter of Genesis is not a scientific account of the beginning of things, and yet it is scientific to the extent that properly understood along with a science properly understood, it is not untrue to the deepest of man's scientific investigations.

The Nature of Man

We are particularly interested here, of course, in thinking about the nature of man and the sin of man and what his opportunities now are in his sinful condition. In the second chapter of Genesis man is described as being made out of the dust of the earth, and we can understand this and agree with it. Man is elemental stuff, and the stuff of his make-up can be listed in the table of elements of a chemist. We know that he is elemental stuff because his body is supported by the food he eats, and in his death he returns to the earth from which he has come.

At the same time we are told two other things about man: that he is "inbreathed" with "the breath of God," and that he is made "in the image of God."

"Inbreathed" with "the breath of God" means that his elemental stuff is "inspirited." One of the oldest questions in human thought is the relationship between mind and body, or spirit and flesh, or soul and body. It is impossible to think of a man as being merely physical as it is impossible to think of him as being merely spiritual, and it is difficult to think of both things at the same time. Yet in some sense, which is a mystery to us, a man is both body and non-body. To make this simple, although not to solve the mystery, think about a man's brain which can be weighed and measured and a man's thoughts which refuse to be weighed and measured. That brain and thought are interlocked no one can deny, but we are constantly forced to think about two different kinds of things interlocked in a way which is inescapably true and endlessly mysterious. This is the nature of man: he is dust of the earth inspirited, and when a man tries to become merely earthy, he is a perversion of himself. Also, when he tries to become merely spiritual, he is another kind of perversion of what he is supposed to be. It is this marvelous interrelationship of spirit and flesh which is the nature and the mystery and the problem of all mankind.

What is meant by the "image of God" is another question. It is evident on the face of it that "image of God" does not mean that we are in some physical sense the sort of creature that would look like God. God is a spirit, and so it is a little ridiculous to think of ourselves as the image of God because we happen to be six feet tall or have blue eyes or are bearded. Even to try to think about the image of God in such terms is immediately and automatically self-defeating.

It is closer to the truth to remember that God is a spirit. Therefore, we are in the "image of God" in those areas of life which are of the spirit — self-consciousness, self-determination, creativity, moral sense, the ability to abstract, and, if you like, even a sense of humor. Each of us could write his own list of parallels as long as we are true to the principle that we image in the things of the spirit.

We recall, however, that man in his essence, as described in this same second chapter of Genesis, is a combination of spirit and body. We are untrue to what we have first said if we dismiss the body because we are in the image of God who is a spirit. As men, we can neither be dismissed from or be a body or spirit; and, if we cannot think of our image as body since God is a spirit, we cannot think of our image as spirit since we do have bodies. How, then, are we in the "image of God" while still being true to the "Gestalt" of the whole man?

It is of the genius of our Bible that long before the new psychology and such discoveries as Gestalt, the Scriptures were already speaking about the *whole* man. It is significant also that when the resurrection became a clear doctrine of the church, it was not so much a question of the immortality of the soul as it was of the resurrection of the body, the body again being the whole man. How then does such a man in the fullness of his humanity exhibit the image of God?

It seems to me that Emil Brunner was on the right trail when he insisted that the "image of God" ought to be a verb instead of a noun. It is not so much what we *are* as what we *do*. The image of God means to "*image*" God. As creatures of God, we are obedient to Him. We are dependent and contingent, and the lines of our life run constantly in His direction or we are in real trouble. The creature cannot and must not break away or try to break away from the sources of his power and life. We recall that Christ perfectly imaged God (and this is something of the meaning of the term "the son of God"), and it was Christ who said of Himself, "My meat and drink is to do my Father's will." The words of Paul have their echo here also, "It is no longer I that live, but Christ that liveth in me"; and again, "For me to live is Christ." The image of God, in short, is a matter of a living, personal, obedient relationship, creature to Creator; and it is only when we are in that relationship that we are in any sense in the image of God.

These words which are given here in such brief explanation have had, as most people know, a long history of scholarly study and comment, but the main lines of what we have said here are clear enough to indicate that man is a special invention, a special sort of creation, a special kind of being. He is this kind of being in a delicate harmony of body and spirit in a special relationship to One whom he has increasingly learned to call Father.

The Fact of Sin

It is only on the background of this understanding that we can fully understand what we mean by the subject of sin. The third chapter of Genesis is again an apparently simple story of what happened in a garden to a man and a woman and a serpent.

Anyone can get the story, but can we get the truth? Sin entered into the world in the form of a serpent, but we cannot understand the meaning of the serpent unless we immediately recognize that the serpent is the enemy of God and man, the adversary Satan. Sometimes we confuse the Bible account with what has worked its way into our thinking by way of such treatments as that of Milton in *Paradise Lost.* Milton goes into much detail with much highly inspired poetic embroidery. But he does not solve the basic question of how evil and sin came into being. He pushes it back a stage to the fall of Satan from heaven, but he cannot make clear to us, as no poet or philosopher has ever been able to make clear to us, why Satan at that early stage chose to rebel against the Almighty. As far as we know, there is no account anywhere, authentic or imaginative, that gives any answer to the problem of the *beginning* of sin. The Bible tells us that sin glides on to the stage of history already full-blown and full-grown. Milton tells us that Satan fell because of pride, but he cannot explain how pride got into Satan, so that the mystery of evil and sin and suffering and death has no answer in terms of its origin.

But we do get a clue in the third chapter of Genesis of how it gets underway. We are given a picture of paradise in the Garden of Eden, and two people living in that paradise in perfect obedience; and, therefore, in perfect harmony with their Creator. They are indeed imaging God. Their communion with Him and their communion with one another are both clear, easy, natural, and enjoyable. This is indeed "bliss beyond compare."

Then things fall apart. We must not allow the simplicity of this story to blind us to the fact that what took place had cosmic significance. As Milton says in *Paradise Lost,* "All creation trembled."

Eve entered into a conversation with evil (this is always the starting place). She entertained the possibility that there might be some other way than God's way. The center of the temptation story is in the appeal of Satan, "Ye shall be as gods." This god role is no role for the creature to take upon himself. There is already a God, and the fulfillment of man's life is in his relationship to that God. The relationship is obedience (the image), and in that obedience is his only hope for growth and felicity. But somehow Eve was led to believe that in the words, "Ye shall be as gods, knowing good and evil," there was a way of life that could run independent of the ground of her being, her necessary line of communication with the source and sustainer of her life. One needs little imagination to recognize that the same thing happens to man now. He enters into a conversation with evil; he figures out that there must be some other way to run things than God's way, and so he makes the effort to break loose from God because, even though God has pronounced judgment on good and evil, he is tempted to be a god himself, "knowing good and evil." But he never knows enough. Only God can see the end from the beginning. Only He can see the whole picture, and men wake up to discover, as Adam and Eve discovered, that, when they tried their own way, they suddenly found themselves under judgment – and outside the garden. There is no going back to the garden with its secrets in the tree of life except past the flaming swords, and I suppose the flaming swords mean utter purification.

Sin, then, is not so much an act or series of acts. Some people sin plain and some sin fancy. We think of ourselves as committing decent sins or superficial sins or pardonable sins, while other people commit gutter sins. We have clean sins and the great unwashed have dirty sins. This is not what the Bible says. The Bible says that sin is a considered attempt to rebel against God's complete will in our life and a willful attempt to set up our own center of operation. God-centeredness becomes self-centeredness, and the means in which we express this selfishness can be almost endless in their variations and possibilities and results. It is at this center that something has happened to the image of God and the delicate harmony between body and spirit is thus badly jarred loose. Milton, with his usual depth in these matters, shows that when man breaks the order of creation between himself and God, he breaks the order of his own life. Significantly this disharmony between creator and creature is a center for all other kinds of disharmonies. This is why Paul suggests in his letter to the Romans "that the whole creation groans," and its groaning continues while it waits the obedience again of men. This is why the poet suggests that "every aspect pleases and only man is vile"; and when man moves into nature around him, he carries with him and within him a disharmony which is destructive of the whole harmony of nature. It may well be legend that St. Francis was clustered about by the birds and small animals, but the legend has truth in it; for, as Francis became increasingly obedient to God, he became increasingly a center of harmony for the nature around him. It is not nonsense to accept literally the words of Isaiah that the "lion and the lamb shall lie down together and a little child shall lead them," if we believe that the fall of man meant disharmony in nature and that the return of man will bring harmony again.

Psychology's Contribution

Modern psychology has done much to support what we are saying. When a man falls apart, it is the language of modern psychology that he has a "schizo" or a split. He suffers from divided loyalties. Instead of harmony he has disharmony. He disintegrates. "Integer" means one, and to "dis-integer" means that the singleness at the center of life has been badly split. Integrity has the same root idea of oneness. It was Paul who said that in spite of everything that tended to break him or pull him apart he had learned to be "content," which is simply the English word for the Latin *contenio* which literally means "held together." The disintegration of individuals and the disintegration of cultures and nations is a normal outgrowth of what we mean by sin. Thus it is that Jesus says, "If . . . thine eye be single, thy whole body shall be full of light. But if thine eye be evil, thy whole body shall be full of darkness." Notice that He says here that the opposite of singleness is not doubleness, the opposite of singleness is evil.

The usual Greek word for sin in the New Testament is *hamartia*, which means "missing the mark," and we miss the mark because we have our eye on two targets at once. Our necessary relationship to our Creator is to life itself, to our very existence; and our self-chosen center of operation rests in our own wills. We try to go down two roads at once, and eventually we are pulled apart. In sum, sin is not an act but a condition. It is not essentially what we do, but it is essentially what we are. It is something that has happened to a relationship. This understanding gets us away from carping and nagging about what other people do or what other people ought to do, and gets us back to the question of their supreme and central loyalty which governs eventually all their doings. This is why the Bible talks about new birth, or our being "a new creation in Christ Jesus," or again, "Out of it [the heart] are the issues of life," or again, "Create in me a clean heart . . . and renew a right spirit within me."

It seems to me that a great deal of discussion and much misunderstanding could be eliminated if we could get back to the core of interpretation at the heart of man's problem and the nature of its solution. As will be indicated in a later chapter, this is the sort of thing that a Saviour came to do, not so much to clean up our sins as to change our relationship; and perhaps we can understand the whole idea of the Gospel better if we can be clear in our understanding of sin.

What gives a special turn to this idea of sin in Presbyterian doctrine is the belief held in the Reformed tradition that there is a continuity in the race represented in the headship of Adam and reconstituted later in the headship of Christ, "As in Adam all died, so in Christ shall all be made alive."

Adam's Part in It All

The Westminster divines thought of Adam as a single person and the head of the whole race, and this one may clearly see from the Scriptures. There are others who have held that Adam is a generic or group name meaning simply mankind. With either interpretation one is saying that mankind as such suffers from this rebellion and that rebellion is the sort of thing that is now normal and natural and "reasonable" to man. There are harsh words about this in our theologies, words like "original sin" and "total depravity."

Original sin does not mean that there is anything particularly "original" about the way we sin. It means more exactly that because of our *nature* all the acts which we commit are at their *origin* in some measure sinful. Even if we attempt to do a completely virtuous or even sacrificial act, we find it impossible to do so entirely for God's sake or for the sake of our neighbor. We eventually illustrate this essential selfishness when people refuse to give us sufficient credit for our goodness, or answer our gifts with ingratitude, or are not even aware that we are as good as we think they ought to know us to be. There are those who argue that we cannot do a perfectly loving act.

I find myself lining up with those of the Reformed tradition, for as honestly as I know myself, I discover in the last analysis, that even the best things that I attempt are already discolored at their origin and their origin is in me. I suffer, indeed, from original sin. I find this condition in me quite inescapable; and, if I watch my self closely enough, I know that I have all kinds of subtle rationalizations and justifications and excuses. It is not surprising, therefore, that I read in the third chapter of Genesis that the serpent was the most subtle beast in the garden.

"Total depravity" does not mean that I am a mad man or that some lovely child in the nursery is "depraved" in any insane sense. What this term means is that this sin at the origin of every act is the kind of depravity that affects my *total* being. In other words, if sin were blue in color all of us would be some shade of blue and maybe spotted here and there in spirit or in body with deeper shades.

Here is where Freud has helped us. There is something desperately wrong with man as man, in the deeps of his nature, in his origins. This is where Jung has helped us. What is wrong with us seems to have a racial continuity. Both agree that we use every possible subtle device to deal with or cover up our true condition. We will not admit to our friends what we are, and we do everything we can so as not to face it ourselves. Whatever charity we might want to express in passing judgment on our friends, we know that such charity will simply not stand up in our own lives when we are honest with ourselves. It is desperately difficult to be honest with ourselves because our honesty itself is discolored at its origins.

As a lovely child will get dirty instead of clean, will tend to get sick instead of well, will slide easily into immorality and have to fight desperately to attain morality, so we have to admit that however lovely things may appear in our endless hopes of improvement there is death in us. However bright our vision may be it is of our nature to skid away from it. It takes something special to keep us heading toward light or truth. As John Calvin says, it is easier to run *out* of the way than to walk *in* it. Or, as Jesus says, "Broad is the way that leads to destruction." How easy it is to scuttle the high demands of the Sermon on the Mount – turn the other cheek, go the second mile, give the coat and the cloak also – by saying, "That sort of living is against nature." How right we are! That sort of living demands a new nature, and this fundamentally is what the Gospel is all about.

Presbyterian doctrine teaches the central headship of Adam and the central headship of Christ, and we are participants in the one by nature and may become participants in the other by grace. The mortal man is a fallen man, and this fact is quite inescapable for all of us in any generation regardless of our intelligence or wealth or the civilization of our culture. Thus there is death in all of us and there is death in what we try to do. God must act to save us or we are lost.

This is where we come to the hard turning point in what happens to individual men and may happen to all mankind. It is at this point that Calvinism and Presbyterianism take their characteristic turn and reveal their characteristic emphasis when they speak of man's eternal destiny for heaven or hell. What they say may appear at first to be offensive. We can only insist that minds of the order of Augustine and Luther and Calvin and Jonathan Edwards have found predestinarian thinking quite inescapable.

Let me turn aside for a moment to an illustration from the college classroom. It is generally agreed that if enough students are included, grades will fall on some kind of a "curve." This means for experienced teachers that if there are several thousand students, the likelihood is that there will be a certain percentage of A's and a certain percentage of F's in that total number. One system of grading for example, suggests that in a class of 100 students there should be 10 A's, 20 B's, 40 C's, 20 D's, and 10 F's. These curves, of course, are not in any way rigid; but year in and year out something like this seems to prevail. What we have to remember is that the same teacher is teaching the same material in the same way to the whole class. Some get it and some do not. This is just one of the facts of life and is well-known in every school. Are the students in such a classroom bound or free? Is not the material available in equal quantities for all of them? The only way we can argue against this kind of fixity is to move to a deeper level and try to analyze why some students are brighter and some not so bright. But why should these differences in intelligence be so? Because back of the "slow" students are all the pressures of genes and environments and probably many hidden factors. If our concern in these matters is a religious concern, and if we believe that the affairs of men are in some way in the hands of God, it is not too difficult to see how starting with the differences in the classroom and moving backward, we can get back to first causes. We can get back to the will of God. Students have different levels of intelligence *inescapably*.

To see this worked out in religion it is natural to turn to John Calvin himself (and Calvin's *Institutes* move at the outset somewhat along these lines). Calvin thinks of theology as the knowledge of God, but he is concerned primarily not with knowledge *about* God but what we would call *saving knowledge*. One kind of knowledge comes to us through the world of nature, or in history, or in man; and the Bible itself supports this kind of knowledge for "The heavens declare the glory of God." Calvin argues that God has given us sufficient knowledge of Himself in this fashion, but because of our blindness in sin we need special knowledge and this is given in a special revelation which we know as the Holy Scriptures. All men, therefore, have available to them this special revelation of God. Still some men do not find saving knowledge while other men do. It is necessary, therefore, and Calvin insists on this, that the Holy Spirit must use the Scriptures to seal the truth of God in the believer's heart.

The Holy Spirit judging by the results – some men are saved and some are not – apparently works in an effectual way through the Scriptures on some men but not on others. This effectual way is called in the Westminster Confession "effectual calling," and since some men are called in a saving way and some apparently are not so called, it is easy for Calvin to take the next step and insist that some men are elected to salvation and some are not.

This is not merely a matter of irresistible logic; Calvin has considerable Scripture on his side. Take for just one example, "No man cometh unto me except the Father draw him." It can be argued on the other hand that the Gospel is offered to "whosoever will." The fact of the matter is, however, that some will and some will not. Calvin finds himself forced by the best logic he can muster to the conclusion that in the last analysis men respond or do not respond to the Gospel call depending on the effectual work of the Holy Spirit through the Scriptures *beyond* what men might learn from nature. It is very difficult from either the observation of life, or the testimony of Scripture, or the logic of a man like Calvin, to escape the idea that man is saved because God wills to work effectively in him by the Spirit and is lost because God does not so will it. This whole system, of course, is built on the assumption that all men are lost in sin through Adam or by virtue of their participation in common humanity, and that salvation is something extra that God has to do and apparently does do for the elect.

It is not my purpose here to argue this but simply to make as plain as possible how this position is reached in Calvinism and Presbyterian doctrine. I am sure that most practicing Presbyterians do not really believe this, but in all candor we must admit that most Christians have not really carefully thought this through.

Jonathan Edwards, the great American theologian, was in agreement with this basic thinking, running from Paul and Augustine through Calvin. Jonathan Edwards puts his special emphasis on the freedom of the will in his work by that name. His reasoning goes something like this. There is such a thing as theoretical freedom of choice, but the question is whether there is actual freedom of choice. I am not free, for example, to jump eight feet in the air. I am not free to be black instead of white nor a medieval instead of a twentieth-century man. On the deeper level I am not *free* of sin therefore I am not really *free* to live without sin. Jonathan Edwards throws the weight of his argument on the side of our inability to do right. As Paul did suggest, even our righteousness is as filthy rags. We are back again to original sin and total depravity.

It is quite unfair to touch on such a marvelous work as Jonathan Edward's *Freedom of the Will* just in passing, but at least we can see again what it is that gives rise to his kind of thinking. In short, unless God gives us His gift of a new birth, unless there is a new creation in us, a new principle of operation, then all our so-called free choices are still caught in the morass of our lost condition. People who argue against this very point would do well to read Jonathan Edwards before being sure that they have really looked into the matter with any seriousness.

This, then, is the Presbyterian view of sin — and freedom — lost men are bound by sin. Only God can really free from sin, and it is only in "new" life that man can be free at all. This is why a modern theologian such as Reinhold Niebuhr says so plainly in many of his works that all men's systems are under judgment. God is not necessarily more interested in the success of godless democracy than He is in the failure of godless communism; both systems or any new system await the new man for the creation of the new society.

CHAPTER 3 — *Questions for Discussion*

1. How should one read the opening chapers of Genesis?
2. What is man's complete nature as described in Genesis 2?
3. What do we mean by "image of God" according to Brunner's interpretation?
4. Review the steps by which Eve fell into sin. How is this descriptive of how everyone falls into sin?
5. How should sin be defined?
6. What do we mean by original sin and total depravity?
7. Does the Presbyterian view of sin make sense when we look at the problem from other viewpoints?
8. What is the place of the Holy Spirit in victory over sin?
9. Is a man's will ever free when he is under the power of sin?

Chapter Four

CHRIST THE MEDIATOR

About a century ago Horace Bushnell in one sentence set the limits for any conversation one could have on Jesus Christ: "Who can satisfy himself with anything he can say concerning Jesus Christ?" In Christ, of course, we are at the center of the faith that bears His name. The central act of His life wrought out man's redemption; yet it is not only the cross but the whole story that is of significance to us — His life from all eternity, His miraculous birth, His Living Word in everything that He did, His wonderful words of life, His death, His Resurrection, His Ascension, and finally what we so frequently forget, His continual intercession for us. With such a sweep of possibilities and even assuming that we are qualified to say what should be said, it is quite evident that what we say will be marked more by what is left out than by what is put in.

There is unanimous agreement among all the churches regarding the centrality of Christ, and it is rather difficult to decide what we should emphasize. For Presbyterian belief, perhaps what I say here is simply reflecting what one Presbyterian has been led to believe to be most important; and to the extent that this reflects the system of doctrine of the Westminster divines, to that extent it is entirely Presbyterian. Necessarily, some things will not be clear and others may be difficult to understand. This is to be expected, for we are attempting to plumb the deeps of God and man, sin and salvation.

God and Man

God and man is the first difficulty. The earliest creeds insisted that Jesus Christ was fully God and fully man and was and is at the same time such a combination of both that we must not emphasize one side of His nature at the expense of the other, nor are we to weld them together in such fashion that we lose sight of either of His natures. Early in the history of the church the creed makers discovered that they must reflect what the Bible says; namely, "that he is fully God and fully man," and however mysterious this may prove or however foreign to normal uses of logic the facts must stand.

We discover in the Scriptural treatment of Jesus Christ that we are dealing with one Person and yet are constantly dealing with two natures, a mystery but not necessarily a conflict. The life of Christ as reflected in the gospels and as explained in the epistles is not the life of some monstrosity as it might be if we should attempt to unite two natures in one person. On the contrary the gospels reflect in their treatment the most attractive figure in all history. At the same time, and this is more than passing strange, one looks to the gospels and the person of Jesus to see what man really is and at the same time looks at the person of Christ to see what God essentially is. How these two natures are together or can be put together beggars any explanation, and interestingly enough the Bible gives us none. The two ideas, the two realities, stand on their own merits; and at the same time we find ourselves dealing with one person.

The story of Jesus Christ in the Scriptures operates constantly on two levels. A baby is born in Bethlehem. A boy grows up in Nazareth. A prophet is baptized in the Jordan River. A teacher reaches great popularity. A leader runs afoul of the forces of the church and the state. A prisoner is crucified and

His followers are scattered. What a tragedy it is that this should happen to the One who "went about doing good." What a tragedy it is that such a teacher should be so far ahead of His day that the only solution they would have for Him is to destroy Him. It sounds almost like another accounting of the life and death of a hero martyr like Socrates.

But there is still that second level in the account. The angels sang at His birth which was birth from a virgin. At the age of twelve He was conscious of being in His "Father's house." There was a voice from heaven at His baptism. There were miraculous powers and a scene of transfiguration. He taught with authority and not as one of the scribes even though He had never had a formal education. And He made amazing claims regarding His own person, which claims were true or the illusions of a mad man, and yet somehow neither the gospels nor the subsequent history will sustain any theory of madness. It was no ordinary crucifixion, for He had told His followers that it must come to pass and tried even before the event to explain something of its meaning. In the hour of His death there were strange phenomena in the heavens and on the earth, and a centurion who had seen many men die said, "Surely this was a son of God." The end of the matter, according to those who knew Him best, and told what they knew about Him while still accepting His claim that He was the truth, was a story of a resurrection and finally of an ascension with the very remarkable words, "All power has been given to me in heaven and in earth," followed by the command that we know now as the Great Commission. Thus the second level is the level of deity.

How could both natures be true at the same time in one person? How could both stories go along together without any apparent strain among those who observed Him and among those of us who read about Him? Jesus Christ is, of course, unique, which means that there are no parallels and no analogies, but there may be some help in observing our own natures. We are accustomed to the way we operate; but when we think about it, there is an essential mystery in the makeup of our own persons which might throw some understanding on the mystery of His person.

The Nature of Man

One of the oldest questions of human thought regarding the nature of man is how two apparently contrary realities make for his personality. We are bodies, made up of matter. We are elemental stuff, of the earth, "earthy." There is no question about our physical nature. At the same time there is a spiritual quality about our lives, some ability even to observe ourselves who are the observers. We have self-consciousness and self-determination, the power of abstraction, a kind of over-all look at things which gives us our sense of humor, qualities which are sometimes called transcendental.

Perhaps the easiest way to see is to think of the differences between our brains which are fully physical and our thoughts which in some way are related to our brains but which at the same time are able to think about our brains and to think about the thoughts themselves. How we think affects our bodies. What happens to our bodies can affect how we think. Sometimes the two seem to work separately. At other times they seem to be interlocked. When someone smiles at us, we see the physical signs in the smile; and yet we know the happiness which the smile suggests for a reality of itself which may or may not show itself in the smile. When we learn a piece of music our eyes are focused on the notes and our fingers are forced to their disciplines. When we have memorized the piece of music, we play automatically – merely physically; and, at the same time, if and when we wish, we may fit into our playing feeling and interpretation and thoughtfulness. While doing so it is possible for our thoughts to move away in imagination and in memory to other things, thus giving to the whole experience something beyond and above anything that is merely physical. A materialist would say the violin solo is the scraping of the hair of a horse over the stomach of a sheep, and naturally considered, that is all it is; but no one who listens to a performance on the violin or attempts to give one ever thinks thus of it. There is the creativity of the composer, the artistry of the violin maker, the possible interpretations in the mind and heart of the performer, and the appreciation of the listener. And the listener can go away from it elevated and motivated because of what has happened.

On a deeper level emotionally we might ask ourselves what happens when we engage in what we call self-examination. A man does not have to be a split personality in order to subject himself to *self*-examination, to pass a judgment on himself, for example, that from this day forward things must be different. Here, even in the leadership of the spirit, there is this kind of plurality and unity, one thing over against another, operating in a mysterious fashion and yet well-known to all of us. That life is mysterious no man can properly deny. That the Person of Christ is a mystery of a like order should not make our acceptance of it an intellectual possibility. We live in such mystery with ease and acceptance every conscious moment.

It is to the credit of those who wrote our early creeds and to the writers of the Westminster Confession that they made no attempt to resolve the mysteries by playing down one side of Christ's person to elevate another. As a matter of fact, our heresies in the history of the church regarding Christ's person have taken sides regarding one or another of His two natures. They have emphasized His manhood at the expense of His deity, or they have so separated His two natures as to make Him a double person, or they have so united them as to lose sight of His two natures. The core of orthodoxy which has run through all the great creeds of the church, and here we repeat, insists that He is fully God and fully man; and we must not divide His person nor confuse His natures.

In passing it is good to suggest here that what we find unique in Christ may be a clue to much more of the nature of things than we ordinarily suspect. It is a clue to the Trinity which speaks of one God and three persons. It is the clue to the sacraments which speak of them as "physical signs of spiritual realities" (and in this sense perhaps all life is sacramental, a display in physical form of things that are spiritually deeper than mere physical appearances), and I think it may well give the clue to what we mean by the Holy Scriptures, what God has to say in man's speech.

It is because of this dual nature that we come to some understanding of Christ as mediator. Here again we must move in the deeps. We must be very clear that Christ took upon Himself human nature, humanity, and we must think about humanity for a moment.

For a simple illustration imagine that there are twenty people in a room, each in turn fully human, and in some sense in the twenty people there is a certain amount if humanity. We could see, I think, that this social group is fully human. Now let the people in the room depart one at a time. We have nineteen in the room now. Do we have less humanity when we have less people? Has the human nature in the room in some sense been minimized? I think not, and this will be perfectly clear when the room is emptied except for the last person. This last person is still fully human. He *has* human nature. Look at him and see human nature. The philosophers have certainly wrestled with this one for centuries, but I think the residue of their thinking is valid. There are realities such as human nature which are not multiplied nor divided. They are of a different order from "things." Is it possible, for example, for a mother to love two children as fully as she loves one? or to love twelve children? Is love the sort of thing that can be multiplied or divided? What shall we do about beauty? Cannot one thing be beautiful? Do twenty beautiful things mean that we are talking about something that is multiplied or is it not rather a reality that is being illustrated in more ways?

Christ's Humanity

What the theologians have been trying to say, and we must not deny the truth of it even if they say it badly (of which this explanation may be a good illustration!), is that Christ in order to be fully man had to *have* human nature. He had to pick up humanity. The Scriptures say that He lived as a human being without sin. The other side of this problem has already been suggested, that human nature sinned in Adam, is now and of itself sinful. Part of Christ's saving work, therefore, is that in taking humanity on Himself and living a life of perfect obedience in the flesh, something new has been added to the human situation. When His life includes human nature our human nature is joined to His. It is the possibility of what we might describe as a blood transfusion. The badness in us is absorbed into the goodness in Him, and His goodness infuses us.

There is, of course, more to it than this. He is called a mediator, not just because He stands in this middle position between the perfection of God and the imperfection of man, but because also in His perfect obedience He wrought out on the cross that which in some fashion satisfied the righteous and just demands of God against sinful man, and at the same time satisfied man that everything that could be done in paying the price for sin was paid by Him, the God-Man.

Anselm stated it something like this: Man sinned against God and could not pay, and God, who could pay, had not sinned. Therefore, it is only in Jesus Christ, the God-Man, that there was one great enough to pay the price who, nevertheless, had in Him the humanity that owed the debt but could not pay.

From the first century on, and this includes the writings of the apostles, what Christ did on the cross has been explained in a wide variety of ways. He gives us an example that we should follow. We are impressed with what He did for us because we couldn't do it for ourselves. Fulfilling the law which man had broken, He satisfied the demands of absolute holiness and justice. He entered into the lists as the champion of humanity. Whatever way we express it, He paid the price. He was the substitute. He satisfied God and He satisfied man. He defeated the powers of evil. What He did was vicarious, substitutionary, complete satisfaction, once and for all.

These matters are discussed at length under various headings in all systematic treatments of theology. What we must be careful to do is to make sure of at least three things: One, that God's justice was satisfied; two, that man's guilt was answered; and three, that Christ stood in our stead to do what we could not do for ourselves. All theologians with any depth at all must circulate around these basic ideas.

One other thing. Paul in II Corinthians says (II Corinthians 5:4), "God was in Christ reconciling the world to himself." Whatever it was that took place on the cross, God was in it all the way. We have no separation here between a harsh God and a loving Son of God. The Son is the full expression of the Father. What we find exhibited on the cross, which is far beyond our power to explain or define, is God Himself, for love's sake absorbing the price, covering the sin and guilt. As P. T. Forsyth has stated, "All the desperate tides of the world's great sins were forced through the channel of a single heart," and that heart was God's heart in the flesh. God was in it all the way and this was something about the way God is and, therefore, something about the nature of the beginnings and the endings and the ground of all reality. We live in a universe, the clue to which is a God revealed in Christ on the cross.

Christ's Classic Offices

To take another turn, the writers of the Westminster Confession bring up again the three classic offices of Christ: Christ as prophet, priest, and king. We remind ourselves again that much more can be said of Jesus Christ than has been said, certainly much more than can be said in such a treatment as this. We follow these three offices of Christ, not because they are exhaustive, but because they serve as a means for summing up briefly and simply what it was He did and what it is He does.

Look first of all at Christ as prophet. What do we mean by a prophet? Normally we mean a man who foretells the future like a weather prophet or like some sports writers telling us how the National League will turn out next season. Without denying this idea in the word, prophet, we must give it a much broader significance. A prophet not only *foretells* as is usually said, but he *forth-tells.* That is, he speaks out. It we take the first part of the word "pro" (although this is not actually the history of the word itself), we get some help here. We use some such expression, pro-German, or pro-Communist, to show that someone stands for someone or something else. It will help us to use "pro" in the same sense when we speak of a *Pro*phet. The prophet is "pro-God." He speaks out (forth-tells) for God.

It seems to me that any prophet engages in at least four things while speaking for God. One, he points to a situation; two, he urges reform; three, he threatens judgment if the reform does not come to pass; four, he again prophesies that which will come to pass regardless of what is done. I might point out, for example, speaking prophetically in this sense, that more money is spent in Washington, D.C. on narcotics than on education. I can further point out that this is a bad situation and that it ought to be reformed, and I think I can further point out that if this kind of ratio of spending is not changed we are heading for real trouble. There is something basically wrong with our society that will have its own pay-off. I could go on to point out, moreover, that should Washington and our own beloved country fall apart, mankind will still have fulfillment without us.

Now all of this is observation on my part and may reflect considerable insights as I have been following more or less the outline of what a prophet does. But the prophet who is "for-God" speaks these same things always from God's viewpoint, not from his own, and he is able to say authoritatively what I can only surmise; namely, the word of judgment and finally the word of promise.

It is in this sense and in another way that I shall shortly suggest that Christ is a prophet of God. Over and over again He insists that He does not speak from Himself but speaks from God. The words that He speaks are not His own. They are God's words, and He speaks as we have suggested, an alarming word of appeal to mend our ways. He speaks a word of harsh judgment on those who do not repent, and He speaks a word of glorious promise that somehow God's will is to be done on earth even as it is in heaven. But something else happens. Christ not only *speaks* the words. He *is* the Word. "He that has seen me has seen the Father"; or again, "I am the way, the truth, and the life." As a prophet He fulfills His office in a double way. He is the living Word; and when we see Him, we know the truth of God; and at the same time He speaks the wonderful words of life, and we hear the truth of God.

This same double nature is seen in Him as He fulfills the office of priest. When Jesus began His ministry, John the Baptist announced His entrance on His ministry in these words, "Behold the lamb of God that taketh away the sin of the world." Christ came as an offering. The lamb was already slain "from the foundation of the world," but He also came as the offeror. "No man takes my life from me. I lay it down of myself." For this cause He had come.

We have already suggested the many ways in which the offering of Christ fulfilled the requirements for our redemption. What we are saying here is that this offering was a self-offering. Christ as priest not only was the offering, but He was the offeror. The priest now does not use something else. He redeems by using Himself.

Look at Christ the King and see this same interesting doubling. Kingship among the nations and throughout history is an interesting study. What are the rights of kings? What are the rights of their person? Back in the time of Samuel and Saul in the beginning of Biblical kingship, we recognize how carefully the subject was protected from misuses. And yet in spite of this it was not long in the history of the Israelites until they had virtually an oriental potentate in Solomon whose kingship was literally a series of demands on his people. Among the prophets in the Old Testament, and especially in Isaiah, we begin to hear something about a suffering servant, and we get the impression from Isaiah that this suffering servant may well have been the king himself. At the same time you hear the glorious words of kingship, "His name shall be called Wonderful, Counselor, Mighty God, Everlasting Father, Prince of Peace. Of the increase of his government and of peace there will be no end." Kingship is more than giving orders.

It seems perfectly evident in the gospels that Christ is a king by virtue of His power and greatness. In short He is glorious because He is kingly. And yet as king He is servant. Hear His words, "If any would be great among you, let him be servant of all." Look especially at the opening of the thirteenth chapter of the gospel according to John, and hear these words, "Jesus knowing that the Father had given all things into his hands, and that he was come from God, and went to God . . . ." Here His deity is expressed in the highest possible terms. Then comes the surprise, indeed the judgment of the Gospel on all forms of power. It was this One of kingly rights who took a towel and girded Himself, put water in a basin and washed the disciples' feet. Paul reflects the same thing in Philippians 2. Here he describes Jesus as being on an equality with God, nevertheless emptying Himself all the way to the death of the cross. Whatever is meant by the kingship of Christ, it is kingship by virtue of and as an essential kingliness of nature which finally and completely serves His people. To put it in other words, He is the shepherd king, the leader, the protector, the one in charge, and yet in the last analysis, "the good shepherd lays down his life for his sheep." In our day, kingship is having a hard time and can justify itself only in terms of service. We shall discover eventually, I am sure, that he who is great among us must be servant of all.

Thus Christ is prophet, priest, and king, a prophet who speaks the word and is the Word, a priest who makes the offering and is the offering, and a king who rules finally in complete self-giving.

The Nature of the Atonement

And now we have to take a hard turn if we are to be true to the theological tradition of Augustine, Calvin, Edwards and the like. It is of the nature of Calvinism and of the Westminster Confession and, therefore, of Presbyterianism that what was accomplished in Christ's mediation must somehow be spoken of as "limited atonement." Is Christ's work somehow insufficient? Not at all, says the Calvinist. The work of Christ is *sufficient.* The question is for whom is it *efficient.* We are thrown back again on that moot question discussed in Chapter 3 where we dealt with man's freedom. Again we must remind ourselves that simple observation of men and their responses or lack of responses to the Gospel leaves us with no other alternative than this; some men do respond and some do not. The Gospel offered is for all men. "Whosoever will, let him come." In such terms the work of Christ is sufficient. The gospels are full of "whosoever" passages. "If any man will hear my voice and open the door, I will come in to him." This emphasis is clear and unmistakable.

The Scripture is equally clear that it is by this work of the Holy Spirit that the words of Christ and the work of Christ are sealed in the hearts of believers. In the saving act God is the initiator of whatever it is that we do and He sustains us in what we do. All is of God. This was battled out by Augustine over against Pelagius centuries ago. It was sustained in characteristic fashion by John Calvin. It was the center of Calvinism versus Arminianism. It is a distinctive in Presbyterianism when Presbyterianism is true to its basic creeds. We have here an unalterable mystery but one which is made unalterably clear in the writings of the gospels, in the emphasis of Paul, and surely in the creeds of the Presbyterian tradition. This is not to say that all Presbyterians hold to this, and it is frequently true that in any discussion on theology Presbyterians along with others will argue vociferously against the idea that everything is of God. "What then is man's choice? What then is man's part in his salvation?" To hear Calvin or the Westminster divines says, "absolutely nothing," is a blow to a man's pride as it is to his logic. Admitting that masses of Presbtyerians do not think along these lines and might even deny this position if they were forced to it, we are equally required to say that this is one of the distinctives of Presbyterianism, that the Gospel is freely offered to all but is efficacious, that is, effective, only to the elect.

Emil Brunner, a Barthian and a man who thought of himself as theologically in the Reformed tradition, tried to turn the edge of this by suggesting that the Bible speaks of election to salvation but does not speak of election to damnation, and that Presbyterians have forced this idea according to their logic and not according to the Scriptures. But Calvin is stubborn at this point. He says to argue in this fashion is a reflection of a "puerile mind." In the history of Calvinism at the Synod of Dort they tried to turn the edge of this by speaking of God's "permissive will." He *elects* some to salvation. He *permits* others to go to their self-chosen damnation. It is hard, however, to think of the permissive will of an Almighty God. Is not the permission of One who holds all things in His hands the same thing as willing what comes to pass?

I make no attempt to justify "the ways of God to man" as Milton set out to do. I confess with others how uncomfortable I am in the support of this "damnable decree," and yet along with Calvin I find two facts inescapable: (1) The Scriptures seem to teach the universal offer of the Gospel and the selectivity of those who are saved; and (2) Our observation of man and his responses to the Gospel seems to indicate that something like this selectivity definitely comes to pass. Anyone who has tried to argue a man to salvation knows that nothing happens until the Holy Spirit works. The Holy Spirit works when and where and how He pleases. We must remind ourselves that God, too, is free, and since He is both free and omnipotent He works His work of salvation where He pleases. As both Jeremiah and Paul point out, can the pottery argue against the potter? Perhaps what we have to rethink in the light of Scripture and experience is not so much the universal possibilities of salvation as the *design* that God had in mind when He provided a mediator. As B. B. Warfield once argued, it is not a question of what we wish were true, but a question of what God says is true.

Beyond this point my own thinking is of no particular value unless to say this. As Paul puts it, "Who knows the mind of God?" Yet we can rest in *His* wisdom; and surely, judging by the cross, we may rest in His love. Can we with our finite minds get beyond the curtain into timeless eternity and pass a judgment on what goes on there in terms of infinite wisdom and infinite love? One thing is certain. Every man who hears the word of the Gospel is perfectly aware of the fact that, in his struggle to accept or reject, all his powers are at work; and, as far as he is a person at all, he is aware that he is making a personal and therefore responsible decision.

A great many people have sat up for a great many hours a great many nights trying to resolve what looks from our viewpoint like a hopeless paradox. If it is a paradox, the Bible leaves it at that. We simply cannot have a God who is not absolutely almighty and this means that He is in charge of every little thing as well as every big thing. At the same time, we cannot have a religion in which man is not morally responsible. We have both, and both at the same time, but we do not have the resolution of this impasse. What we do have, and this must be underlined again and again, is the clear experience of our own decision and, when we look at ourselves honestly, a clear understanding that we can choose if we will. Those who say it is all of man and his freedom have left out the greatest dimension in our faith. Those who say that it is all of God in some mechanical fateful way have played fast and loose with their own experience and have forgotten that we are not the objects of deterministic forces but the objects of the love of a personal God. We don't know everything and most times we don't know enough, but we can if we will (and we operate always on this side of the curtain) accept Him whose will is our peace.

CHAPTER 4 — *Questions for Discussion*

1. Describe the nature of Christ as fully God and fully man.
2. Show how this fact is illustrated by the two "levels" of Jesus' life.
3. Do we find a parallel in our own natures to the nature of Christ? How?
4. How is the nature of Christ related to the understanding of the Trinity?
5. According to Anselm why do we need a God-Man as mediator?
6. What kinds of things are settled by Christ's mediation?
7. What are the three offices of Christ?
8. How is Christ both priest and offering?
9. What is meant by limited atonement?
10. What contribution does man make to his own salvation? Explain.

Chapter Five

JUSTIFICATION, SANCTIFICATION AND GOOD WORKS

It is the fashion in theological circles today to lay hold on words which are being used in common talk and apply them to religious ideas. There is a constant attempt to popularize theological language. A better attempt, it seems to me, is to give meaning to the theological words which have served the church for many years. It would be pretty difficult to replace the words justification and sanctification with modern words which would carry the same meaning. Why not give content to the words which we have? Suppose we try.

Both justification and sanctification have one basic idea and an important one. The last part of each word comes from a Latin word which means "to make" (sometimes, "to do"). The form of the word is such that we can think of it in the past tense as something that has been made or something that has been done. The word justification has in it the Latin *jus* or *ius,* which means "just" or "right." And now we have our word justification which means *made right* or *made just.* The word sanctification has in it the Latin *sanctus* which means "holy" or, if you like, "good." The two words, then, in order, mean "made right" and "made holy."

We need now to give attention to what we mean by the phrase "made right." The word is fundamentally a legal term. We are made right in a forensic sense. We are "rightened." It is the rightness that a criminal might have before the bar not because he did not commit the crime, but because someone "made good" for him according to the demands of the law. A man could well owe a sum of money which he could not pay, and he would, therefore, be guilty before the bar; and he could at the same time owe a debt in some form to society. It would be possible then for someone who cared enough about him to pay his fine or to restore what had been stolen and the man would be set free. This would not mean that he was a *good* man or that he was not guilty of the crime charged. It would simply mean that before the bar of justice he is now "justified" or made right. To put it in other words, he has been rightened. This is not a difficult concept to grasp, but what we have to be very clear about is that no change has necessarily taken place in the prisoner's character. He is not personally better nor worse necessarily than he was before. He simply stands in a different relationship to the law, or to the judge, or to society, not because of any merit in him but because the price has been paid to cover his crime.

If we think of this in religious terms, we can begin to get at what theologians from the time of the Apostle Paul have been talking about when they say that we have been justified. The law of God has been broken, and some price certainly must be paid to make satisfaction. Man is guilty as charged in his offenses against God and against God's law, and the enormity of the crime, or of the sin in this case, is measured by the fact that it is a sin against God. The sinner is a rebel. He is in the larger sense a traitor, and according to the whole thrust of the Scriptures he is worthy of death.

To this extent (and there is, of course, much more to the Atonement than this), the death of Christ is the price paid to satisfy the demands of the law, to satisfy the demands of divine justice and to cover the sin against God. We are not defining here what the offense against God has been for we have already talked about that in the chapters on sin and on Christ as Mediator. We are trying to make only one thing clear, that whatever it is that man has done that is worthy of death has been "wholly covered," not by anything he has worked out or any price that he has paid or could possibly pay, but by the price which Christ paid on the cross. We remind ourselves again that this is a forensic term, that is, a legal term, and that it has to do with a legal transaction with God as judge, with the law of God, the sin against God and the price to be paid. This is all a part of the good news, the price has been paid completely once and for all.

We read in Paul that we are "justified by faith." What does that mean in this context?

An Illustration

Let us suppose that I have ordered an expensive meal in a first-class restaurant only to discover that I have no money, no credit card, and apparently no one in the restaurant who knows me or trusts me. The manager of the restaurant gently but firmly points out that there are plenty of dishes in the kitchen waiting for just such a man as I; and since payment is expected, that is the way it will be done. At this point someone else steps up and offers to cover my debt. Notice here that I can either accept or refuse this offer. If I refuse the offer, I am condemned to the dishwashing in the kitchen. But if I accept the offer then I feel that in some sense I am "beholden" to the one who has paid the price. It may well be, and this often happens because of our pride, that we do not want to be "beholden" to anyone. We would rather work out our debts than have someone else cover them, because whenever someone covers our debts we enter into a new relationship with him, and very plainly feel ourselves indebted. Will we accept the gift or will we refuse it? I think this will depend upon whether we do or do not want to owe everything to the one who wants to cover our debts.

We must not let this simple illustration lead us to suspect that we are illustrating a simple thing. The whole point of man's need is that he cannot pay his own debt at all, ever. His has been an infinite offense, and he has only finite abilities. He needs someone to pay the debt who has in him that which is acceptable, not to a restaurant owner, but to Almighty God. Is there anyone good enough to pay the price for sin?

This is something of what it means then when we accept Christ. First of all, we accept God's judgment on our sin. We accept what sin really is from God's viewpoint, not our own. Second, we recognize that we cannot possibly pay. Third, we believe that what is offered to us in Christ in the Gospel is sufficient to cover our need; and fourth, this is very important, we are willing to enter a relationship of gratitude toward the One who has paid the price. You will be impressed, I think, if you work along these lines, to discover how the whole idea of "accepting Christ" involves much more than what would appear on the surface. In some fashion we are accepting the whole thrust of the Gospel, the truth of God, concerning sin, debt, satisfaction, and the whole nature and work of Christ. Do we really believe that all this is true? If we do, it seems to me that we have taken to ourselves a whole world view, a whole slant on reality, and if you like, a philosophy of life. When we are justified therefore it is by this kind of faith, belief in the whole truth, and new life on the new basis.

When we have made this acceptance, the promise is that we stand justified; that is, we are "redeemed" toward God. This is not something we have done but something that has been done. Our only place in the whole transaction has been the acceptance of what has been done. "We bring nothing to our salvation but our sin." Again note that this does not change our natures immediately. We are not better one moment after it happens than we were one moment before. We have simply entered into a new relationship toward God through Christ. To use other language, this is a new birth in the sense of the seed of a new life having been sown. We are at the point of a "new creation." We have reached that point where we are "converted," that is, it is a turning point, a change of direction, the introduction of a new life principle. From here on all things will be different, but they will be different because at the very point something has been done to us and for us to give us a new start.

Some years ago our family stopped at Banff and Lake Louise in Canada, and our children wanted to ride on the ski lift in Banff. Each one of us in turn climbed into the seat ready for the ride to the top. When we climbed into the seat, we were still at the bottom of a very high and dangerous hill which no one of us could have climbed; but, by virtue of being seated in the seat as directed, we were assured of our eventual arrival at the top. We did not control the ski lift in any way but by sitting on the assigned seat, our acceptance of the offered arrangement created an entirely different relationship to the problem of reaching the top of the hill and happily, in due time, we arrived.

Teaching Justification

One thing hard to teach (and I have tried this for many years in the college classroom) and, indeed, one of the hardest things to understand, is this act of justification. The Westminster Shorter Catechism which is based on the Westminster Confession says that justification is an "*act* of God's free grace." It is a thing done, a thing accomplished, and a thing done entirely by God; from this point we now begin to move in a new direction.

The move is from justification to sanctification. Justification means that we are "made right." Sanctification means that we are "made holy." Whereas justification is an *act* of God's free grace, sanctification is a *work* of God's free grace. Justification is an *event*. Sanctification is a *process*. Having been justified, we are in a new relatianship by which we are empowered now to grow in holiness.

To return to the illustration of the ski lift, justification gets us aboard. Sanctification is the ride. The ride can be rocky and windy and apparently quite perilous. There can be, as there were on our ride, pauses, stops and starts. To be even more exact about it than the illustration will allow, the graph that would illustrate the program of a Christian's new Christian life could have many low points as well as many high points, but we understand in the use of a graph that regardless of the high points and the low points there is a trend, a direction, and this direction is constantly up. This is why we can allow in the life of a Christian that many things will be far from perfect. The basic question for the Christian is whether his relationship is right because as long as that is right, regardless of the ups and downs of his religious and moral life, the trend will be constant, and in the right direction.

In so many Christian circles in which I find myself, and it is particularly true in youth conferences and the like, the emphasis is often put upon the question of success, or point of arrival, rather than on the question of relationship. I have heard conference speakers urge young people to act like Christians when the young people were not Christians. We often talk about how a person ought to live before we have any notion of whether he has even been born. We expect a man to be sanctified before he is justified.

Some years ago in the United Nations there was one of those usual desperate conflicts between the Arabs and the Jews over a question in Palestine. An American mediator in his exasperation, and he was more than he knew a reflection of his New England Puritan background, cried out at the litigants, "Why don't you men act like Christians?" At first this sounded reasonable but it wasn't really. The men had no reason to act like Christians because they weren't Christians.

Over and over again we do this; we try to introduce Christian action before we have talked about Christian commitment. We must remind ourselves that justification precedes sanctification. It was John Oman who said, "It is not important what rung we occupy on the ladder; the question is whether we are climbing or falling." People who have studied embryology tell us that at a certain stage in the development it is virtually impossible to tell the difference between a sheep and a pig and a man, but amazing differences are there. Because of the life essence of each, one embryo will grow into a pig and another will grow into a man, and happily for us it is impossible for it to happen any other way. Our Christianity is the seed of new life in us. Christianity is not an attainment but a new nature. It is not a success but a loyalty. It is not something a man can pride himself on, but something he can depend on; what he is and what he is capable of doing is not established in his own wit or his own strength but in the free gift of another's life.

An understanding of justification and sanctification can go a long way toward eliminating our false pride and our judgments on others. If my goodness is not something I myself do for myself, what credit is it to *me?* One churchman observed when he saw a drunk in the ditch, "There but for the grace of God am I," and if Christians really believe what they say they believe that "all is of grace," there simply cannot be any place for pride and surely nothing of that spirit of the Pharisee who said, "I thank thee, God, that I am not like other men, especially that publican."

It is a temptation of mine to recognize easily and with great satisfaction the areas of my life where I have attained some victory and some success. At the same time that I recognize my attainments I tend to excuse or rationalize those areas of my life where I have not attained. And so I look down in judgment on my brother who does not attain in the areas where I attain and on which I pride myself and fail to recognize that he may have tremendous success in those areas which I have minimized because I have not succeeded there myself. I think I can report for the record that I have never stolen anything, but then on the other hand I have never been desperately hungry nor have I seen my children hungry. My tendency, then, is to pass judgment on the thief. His stealing, however, may have been motivated by his largeness of heart; maybe he stole for the sake of others and was willing thereby to lay his own life and soul on the line for the sake of others. Meanwhile, as a Christian who has never been hungry, I have had all kinds of excuses as to why I have not shared a part of what I have with those who are hungry. From the standpoint of the Judge of all the earth it is a nice question as to who of us is under condemnation.

I have known many men who have been under the compulsion of strong drink, and I have known a few alcoholics. This has not been one of my problems, but at the same time it would not take a very clever person to see that some of these men have been driven to drink by personal problems which I have never had. Maybe with their problems I would be driven to drink and, if I am honest with myself, I recognize that they have problems which I have never lifted a hand to help. I have been impressed constantly with the fact that men and women who are drinkers are also, when they are sober, some of the most gentle and concerned people that I know among my friends. They are thoughtful and considerate, and they are fun to be around. And I have some sober friends who are harsh and critical and judgmental. They despise their brother who drinks and somehow manage to hide their own pride and lovelessness.

Being Judgmental

People who really believe in justification and sanctification, that is that we are *made* right and *made* holy, can never really so believe and then move themselves into the position of the judge. They might become brokenhearted over their brother's act but this is an entirely different thing from hate, despising their brother's heartbreak. One of the most marvelous things about Christ's ministry is summed up in the words, "in that while we were yet sinners Christ died for us." There was nothing "going for us" when He made His move. On the other hand if we are not careful, we discover that we can love only "our kind of people," the lovable, or the grateful, the nice people, the kinds of people who commit the decent sins that we commit (usually sins of the spirit like pride and covetousness), who do not commit the so-called gutter sins which we find offensive. It was while men were sinners that Christ died for them. How is it with us?

Some years ago a man named Russell suggested that over the entrance of every church there should be a sign "For Sinners Only." This illustrates what is probably the greatest piece of forgetfulness in the Christian church: every congregation is made up of sinners and nothing else. Some may have been at their Christianity longer than others, some may have been successful in areas where others have failed, and vice versa, but there simply is no one in any church who is not a sinner; and, if we want to come right down to it, it was Paul who said that even "our righteousness is as filthy rags." From the standpoint of the holiness of God even the best of us has in no sense attained to it. This is why Paul can say without any false modesty "sinners of whom I am chief." As a matter of fact, one of the marks of our progress in the Christian faith is an increased sensitivity to the amazing number of areas in which we are sinners. And the other side of this is that we increase in our sympathy for those who are having their own struggles. Why is it that a college student who is taking calculus doesn't dream of condemning a third-grader because he knows only arithmetic, whereas a "successful" Christian will so easily and almost automatically condemn someone who is still a babe in Christ and not yet up to his standards? Again quoting Paul, "What have you that has not been given to you?" Whence then comes our pride? What right have we to move into the seat of the judge? Only God can judge.

In our day it seems to me that we can learn more about this sort of thing from Alcoholics Anonymous than we can from many Christian congregations. Note that a man cannot become a member of Alcoholics Anonymous unless he accepts the fact that he can no longer do anything for himself. Alcoholics Anonymous is made up of men and women who have agreed in themselves and to each other that their weakness is real and fatal and that they simply cannot go it alone. No one belongs to the organization who does not accept his "lost" condition. Then what does the organization do? With complete sympathy for the other man's problem because it is his own problem, every man in the organization stands ready, not to judge his brother (they are all under judgment), but to help his brother day or night at any time and by any means.

We need not think of liquor as a sin or as peculiarly sinful to get the point. What we ought to learn from such an organization is that the church of Jesus Christ is supposed to be *in every regard* what Alcoholics Anonymous is with regard to just one problem. One can hardly imagine what this kind of understanding would do to most congregations, and one can hardly imagine why it is that we have so completely missed the point of our Christian faith and what it means to be saved by grace alone. Every man and woman in the church (and every other man and woman is in the same boat) have said plainly when they took their vows of membership that they need the salvation which only Christ can give. Every man and every woman, therefore, stands ready day or night, in season and out, not to judge (all are under judgment) but to help.

This is where the cross as the symbol of our Holy Faith forces itself into the picture. Most people are well-acquainted with John 3:16. "God so loved the world that he gave his only begotten Son," but move on to John 3:17, "Christ came not to judge the world, but that the world through him might be saved." We take the name of Christ and call ourselves Christians. We come not to judge the world in His name; but, as co-workers with Christ, we are working to redeem the world. And what does Christ say to us? "If any man would be my disciple, let him take up his *cross* and follow me." If a Christian congregation can become a kind of glorified Alcoholics Anonymous, then the only question facing any member of the congregation is this: What price am I willing to pay, what cross am I willing to bear, to redeem the situation in which I find myself? The disciple's cross in the Christian life means that there is no redemption apart from self-giving for the sake of others. This is what Christ did—"while we were yet sinners." This is fundamentally what we are called to do if we are His disciples.

This is a good place to look at a common criticism of the church among those outside the church: that the church is "nothing but a bunch of hypocrites." In some ways this is a fair criticism. In another way it is not. It is a fair criticism if the church is made up of sinners who don't recognize that they are sinners and who, therefore, preen themselves on their successes and explain away their failures—failures which those outside the church can see clearly indeed. The church ought to be under judgment when it becomes nothing better than a community of judges.

In another sense the church can rightly be called "a bunch of hypocrites" and glory in it. If by hypocrisy we mean that a man does not live up to his ideals, then, of course, this is the first thing you can say about any Christian. The ideal is nothing less than perfection, nothing less than the holiness which we see in God revealed in the face of Jesus Christ. Any Christian who lives up to his ideals has somehow missed out on what Christian ideals really are. Every Christian is a spiritual and moral failure in terms of possible Christian goals. To that extent he is a hypocrite, but I am sure that if he recognizes himself as a hypocrite, in such terms or for such reasons, he will not be criticized by the world outside the church for that kind of hypocrisy. Every Christian is in the process of becoming sanctified, that is he is being "made holy"; and, as long as he is in the process, you can be perfectly sure that he is still short of his goal. Perhaps the man outside the church has his own hypocrisy, a reversed hypocrisy if you like. "One thing about me," he says, "I'm no Pharisee." He is dead right. He is no Pharisee, because he has not even tried to keep the law of God, and he is suffering his own kind of the deadly sin of pride. He believes in his own standards of success, by his own choice of standards he has assured his own kind of failure. So he also is in no position to judge. Only God can judge.

In the light of this discussion we can understand why some Christians have been tempted to "antinomianism," which is a long word meaning lawlessness. If all is of God in the initiation and in the sustaining of the Christian life, then there is no one to blame for moral failures except God, so they reason. The Bible, of course, will not allow this kind of moral evasion at all. Paul has an interesting discussion of this sort of thing in Romans. It is because of sin that God must show His grace. Grace is a good thing. Therefore, the more sin, the more grace, so our sin gives opportunity for God's grace, etc. "Shall I sin then," says Paul, "in order that grace may abound?" Then Paul cries out, "God forbid." It is in this kind of reasoning that we show ourselves to be moral rebels. Just because everything is of God we are brought back quickly to the nature of our acceptance of Christ's offer in the first place. Remember here what we said earlier, that the acceptance of Christ's offer is the acceptance of the whole nature of reality as it is revealed through Christ. To accept ourselves as sinners in God's sight and to accept an offer of salvation on God's terms is, by its very nature, a setting of our minds and hearts against sin. That is, one who accepts Christ takes Christ's viewpoint on the nature of sin and the necessity for salvation. In other words, when we are justified at all we have moved over to His side of the battle against lawlessness and sin. And furthermore, if we are in any sense co-workers with Christ (real disciples) in the redemptive process, we can hardly side with the enemy while we are trying to win the battle against the enemy.

We can't have it both ways. Any man who reasons that he can have one side of the coin without the other, that he can accept Christ's verdict on sin and still take a light view of sin, has somehow missed the whole point. As we suggested before, one of the marks of growth and one of the marks of the sanctification process is an increased abhorrence of sin and an increased appreciation of the endless subtle ways we can sin and the infinite effects our sin can have on other people. No man who accepts justification, no man who is interested in being sanctified toward that great day when he will be glorified will ever argue that his sin doesn't matter because, after all, it's God's problem not his own. Heine, the German philosopher, was somewhere nearly right when he said, "God forgives sins. That is His business." This is true. But if we use that truth as an excuse for our immoralities, we have surely scuttled any sensible view of what it means to accept Christ.

"Good Works"

Here now is a good place to discuss what we mean by "good works." In general one of the differences between Romanism and Presbyterianism lies in the interpretation which they put on good works. In some ways the whole structure of the Roman Church stands on the idea of works, merit, penances, and the like. There are things which a man does to *earn* forgiveness. There are things to be done to *assure* salvation. When a Roman Catholic goes to confession he does so with the realization that confession itself is a good work. He recognizes, also, that the church is the storehouse of grace because there have been innumerable saints (and some really good ones like Mary or Peter) who have not only accomplished sufficient works for their own personal salvation but have stored up extra works in the church. These are called works of supererogation. All the saints, the monks in their monasteries, the nuns in their nunneries, live good lives but live such lives that the margin of their goodness is collected to be used elsewhere. Thus it is that when the priest says, "I absolve you," to the confessing sinner, he is able to do this because he draws on the grace the church has preserved in its storehouse of grace.

Many people find no assurance in this sort of thing, and their hearts are not quiet. Luther was a prime example of a monk who could find no satisfaction in his works. How fast does a man have to run? How high does he have to jump? How hard does he have to work to deserve the love of Almighty God? As a matter of human experience, does anyone ever really earn the love of someone else? Does anyone really deserve the grace of one who loves him? Is it not the mark of love everywhere that those who are recipients of love cannot be worthy of the one who loves them? They have in no sense earned it.

It was Luther who emphasized the idea, although he did not start it, that there is no possible way to *earn* salvation. A man must, therefore, accept the free gift. The price has been paid, the sin is wholly covered, the transaction is complete once and for all. We are justified by faith which means that we recognize and accept all that Christ has done and all that Christ stands for.

Once this has been done, however, once this acceptance has been made, our good works are an expression of our new relationship. There is no escape for the Christian from good works, not because they earn his salvation, but because they necessarily express his salvation.

Perhaps all of this is illustrated by friends of ours who adopted a seven-year-old boy (and the Westminster Confession speaks of adoption in connection with justification and sanctification). The boy was playing on a playground at an orphan home, and our friends observed him through the window of one of the buildings. They then chose him for their own apart from any decision or understanding on his part at all. They were able to take him into their home and they gave him their name. Their name meant that officially, legally, and always, he was the rightful participant in the life of that home and the inheritor of its gifts. He in no way earned this, and once it happened to him there was no way he could escape it.

We observed this boy shortly after he had become a part of his new home. He had all kinds of dirty habits, and worse than that some frightful words. Frequently he awoke screaming at night. He was quite insecure in a hundred different ways. This boy now is making an enviable record for himself as a student and as an athlete in a good college. He carries his new name, but he has been learning how to live up to that new name that he bears, and increasingly he brings glory to the household of which he is a part. All of these things he has learned to do, and one of the happy things about his new relationship is that increasingly he has wanted to do the good sort of thing in grateful response to what the love of these parents did for him in the adopting and in the sustaining of his life.

To push the parallel a little farther, these same people adopted a second son when he, too, was about seven years of age. One of the delightful realities in that home now is what the older adopted son has taught the younger son about the meaning of his new relationship and what he has done for this younger boy in trying to express toward him the love which he first received from those parents.

I can think of no greater expression of what it means to be justified and sanctified. I can think of no better perspective in which to put the whole idea of good works. The Christian is one who shares the name of Christ. He belongs to the household of God. There are certain ways of living in such a household; and, when these ways are lived, the new kind of life brings glory to the name of the whole family. Then he wants to tell and show others.

CHAPTER 5 – *Questions for Discussion*

1. Explain the terms justification and sanctification.
2. How do these two terms differ in their meaning?
3. How does Christ justify? How does Christ sanctify?
4. Give some explanation of salvation by "grace alone."
5. Why must justification precede sanctification?
6. How does an understanding of these truths condemn our pride and our harsh judgment of others?
7. Use Alcoholics Anonymous to illustrate what Christianity ought to be.
8. "The church is full of hypocrites." How should this be answered?
9. How do we escape antinomianism?
10. What is the difference between Protestant and Catholic teaching of "good works"?

Chapter Six

CHRISTIAN LIBERTY AND THE LIBERTY OF CONSCIENCE

Although the Bible is considered to be a revelation, it also presents to the thoughtful reader a series of unresolved problems, and none is greater than that represented by the problem of Christian liberty.

The problem is set before us plainly by an answer of Christ and in a statement of Paul.

When the Jewish leaders were attempting to trip Jesus, they used as one of their devices a question concerning His relationship to the Roman state. It was a tricky question. Should one pay tribute to Rome or not? If Jesus answered that tribute should be paid, He would raise serious questions in the minds of the Jews. If He urged that tribute should not be paid, He would lay Himself open for a charge which later was sustained against Him: namely, that of treason. He answered this catch question by a question of His own. He asked them to bring one of the coins of the realm, and then He asked His tormentors whose superscription was on the coin, and they had to answer, "Caesar's." "Render unto Caesar," He said then, "the things that are Caesar's, and unto God the things that are God's."

This was an excellent answer in that it threw the decision back on His questioners. The only trouble for forthcoming generations is that there is still no answer to the question which Jesus posed: namely, what things are Caesar's and what things are God's?

The very fact of the coin should have made quite plain to them as it makes plain to us that the state makes many of its own special gifts to the life of man and, therefore, may require some return from him. The stamp of Caesar's image on the coin gave the coin value, and the value of the coin made possible all kinds of trade inside the Roman Empire. It was the power of the Caesars as well that cleared the seas of pirates and the roads of brigands. It was the power of Caesar that made relatively safe the borders of the empire inside which men and their families were able to carry forward their normal pursuits. It was inside the domain of the Caesars that the very religion that Christ came to found was able to have its start at the registration for taxation at Bethlehem, in the quiet of the carpenter's shop at Nazareth, in the streets of Jerusalem, and in the peaceful hills of Galilee. Neither wars nor insurrections troubled the Founder nor His followers as the memorable words were spoken and the matchless life was lived by which all subsequent generations should be blessed. We know that Jesus Himself could not have pursued His carpentry or carried out His teaching apart from His being a taxpayer to the Roman Empire. If we think of Him in terms of His human personality, then tax paying even to a pagan government and a conquering power was a part of His perfection. Whatever perfect obedience He owed to God He owed something to the State. Later theologians were to talk about the state as an "order" by which life was ordered.

On the other hand, no teacher was more outspoken in His demands for perfect obedience to God: a man's "meat and drink" is to do the will of the Father. Or again, "You are my friends if you do the things which I command you." One of the meanings of cross-bearing among His disciples certainly involved obedience to God even unto death. And we must remind ourselves that, from the human standpoint at least, Christ met His death because He ran afoul, not only of the forces of the Jews, but also the forces of the Roman Empire; and it was in His perfect obedience to God – for this cause He had come – that He was crucified, and the crucifixion was quite impossible apart from the permission of Pilate and the very direct acts of the Roman soldiery.

It is certainly clear therefore that some things are owed to the state. But it is clear also that some things are owed to God. Most of the time these two autonomous demands in a man's life do not conflict, but there is the possibility of a "gray" area where in the conflict between the church and the state a man must make his agonizing decisions.

A case in point in our day would be the decision of a pacifist taking the command, "Thou shalt not kill," as an absolute. The pacifist then decides for himself, and would urge on others, that under this command of God there is no way open to him except to resist the state by refusing to bear arms. He is caught, of course, in an unfortunate situation because, if he stays alive at all, then the food he eats, or the house he lives in, or the jail he inhabits, or the peace work which he finds acceptable, are all related in some way to the very structure of the state which is carrying on the war which he is opposing. If he refuses to eat, he is engaging in self-killing or he may, if he chooses, douse himself with gasoline and burn himself to death as a witness, but once again he has exhibited that in order not to kill, he is killing. He finds it quite impossible to absolutize his insistence on one law, "Thou shalt not kill." At the same time every man, potentially at least, can reach a time under the pressure of the state where he has to say for one reason or another that he can go this far and no farther, and then and there he must make a stand. Luther was not only opposing Rome, but also the emperor when he said, "Here I stand. God help me. I can do no other." The place where each man decides that he must take his stand for God against the state may not be the same place where another man takes his stand, but it requires no great imagination on the part of any of us to see that each man in his own case can very well have that point beyond which the state cannot move him.

What we are saying here is an attempt to make plain that when Jesus gave His answer for Caesar *and* for God He did not tell us where a man's loyalty would finally rest when he had to make a decision *between* Caesar and God.

The same problem is given the same indecisive answer by the Apostle Paul in Romans, "The magistrate does not bear the sword in vain," because "the powers that be are ordained of God"; and the early verses of Romans 14 are to make plain to us that a man should obey the powers of the state as a power ordained of God, and that the magistrate does not bear the sword in vain because the magistrate has the power to enforce even unto death the powers of the state.

The Early Church

The early church found itself in a peculiar relationship to Rome because of what had happened in their day, the Roman emperor being deified and therefore requiring some form of worship. The problem of the early church was not that they had introduced a new religion into the Roman Empire – the Roman Empire was accustomed to all kinds of religions – but the fact that the Christians could not bow down and worship the emperor. How many hundreds were miserably destroyed for this difficult requirement in their Holy Faith. Yet one cannot read the writings of the apostles without reading over and over again that the Christians are to be good citizens, that they are to obey the rulers of a pagan state, and that they are to obey even in enforced loyalty, their only problem being that at that point (whatever that point was) where the state made it impossible for them to obey God they must then resist even unto death.

This paradox of loyalty continued throughout the history of the church and continues to our own day. One gets the impression that Luther with his concern for the Christian nobility and his revulsion against the uprisings of the peasants swung toward obedience to the state. And in the churches of the German tradition or more exactly the Luther tradition, the solution to the church-state problem has fluctuated between the escape from the problem in quietism or pietism or more frequently the willingness to leave the state entirely as many quietistic and pietistic German groups did.

In Calvin, however, and in what is called the Reformed tradition, there evolved eventually the attitude (and this is a study in itself) that unwillingness to have the state make demands on one's religion might lead eventually to a revolt against the state in a revolutionary act to change the state toward some harmony with the will of God. The reasoning was something like this: The powers that be are ordained of God, but if the powers do not act like powers ordained of God, illustrated by their persecution of the people of God, then the people of God have not only the right but also the duty to revolt. This is why in the Calvinistic and Reformed tradition we can find something like the beheading of Charles the First or the revolt in blood of the Covenanters or the Beggars.

Of equal interest, it seems to me, is the fact that in the Germany of Hitler the Lutheran Church found a way to adjust to such a regime. There was even then a state church. The religious revolt against Hitler was carried on primarily by members of the Confessional Church which was in the true Reformed tradition. It has been a mark of a Presbyterian, therefore, in relation to this particular problem, not only that a Christian must be a good citizen and obey the state and also a good Christian and obey God, but that if there is a showdown between these two powers, then and only after an excruciating and agonizing decision he has the right and the duty to revolt. It would be interesting to see how many of the American revolutionists were Scotch-Irish Presbyterians! We recognize, of course, that the American Revolution was not primarily an issue between the state and the church.

The Situation in Our Own Day

In our own day there have been some interesting problems. The American solution to the church-state problem is the separation of church and state. The state is to establish peace and security, and in this sense it is ordained of God in order that inside this peace and security the church may have opportunity to preach the Gospel and to bring men to Christ. In theory this is better than a church-state or a state-church, but it leaves its own problems; and these problems are not far away from the original problem given in Christ's answer to His questioners.

What should the church have done in Japan under the requirements of emperor worship? What should the church do today in a Moslem country where certain requirements toward the state are demanded before the religion is free to operate? What happens over the question of Bible reading in the schools when it can no longer be assumed that the United States is a Protestant country? Have we run into an impossible emphasis in our separation of church and state when by this position we find it impossible to teach any form of religion in our public schools and in most of our colleges and universities? Does the separation of church and state mean that education is supposed to be irreligious? Is this in itself a move by the state to stamp out religion at the very times and places where young people would be expected to believe in or learn the principles of their faith? How do we justify chaplains in the Armed Forces paid by the state? Why does the president take his oath on the Bible? What can be said for putting on a Christmas play or an Easter pageant in a school (and would this even be Christian to insist on) if 80 per cent of the students in the school are Jews? The answers are not clear, and they are not easy, and no new solutions have been forthcoming in spite of the long history of struggle between the church and the state.

The liberty of any man is a precious thing. But it has a peculiar pressure on the Christian because of his insisting on a certain kind of liberty which has to do with his full commitment to God. Presbyterians generally have felt that any solution must involve some kind of pressure by the church on the state. Stringent criticism has been brought to bear on the United Presbyterian Church in our country today because of public church statements made on such subjects as Red China, race, poverty, atomic war, and the like. Those who insist on the church bringing its forces to bear in such fashion (and no one really knows what, if any, force has thus been brought to bear) are in my opinion in the true tradition of Calvinism and Presbyterianism. The powers that be are ordained of God. There is no question of that. The church is established for the salvation of men's souls, and the church should be protected in that.

Nevertheless, and here is where the whole problem gets very binding, when and in what ways should the church bring its power to bear upon the state if it feels certain that what the state is and how the state operates make it quite impossible for the will of God to be done in the society under the power of that state? I am quite satisfied that no one can be too sure of his answers in his own day as we may second guess what has been done in other days. We are in the battle and not above or outside of it, and this is always a confusing position in which to be. Nevertheless it is of the genius of Presbyterians that something must be done.

I have a vivid memory of an evening spent at a delightful dinner in an English home. My wife and I were guests of a university professor and his wife, and it was the awful night of the announcement of the abdication of Edward the Eighth. When this news came over the "wireless" both the professor and his wife became extremely agitated, and in a sense the evening as a social affair never recovered itself. What was significant to me, and is clear in my memory now, was the wife getting up from the table and pacing the floor, apparently unmindful of her guests, as she kept repeating to herself and I suppose to us, "What *should* we do? What *can* we do?" Her automatic reaction was that in a national crisis there was something a Christian should do.

The Presbyterian in general cannot escape this call to duty in his creed, in his history, or in his conscience. Not only must Christians as Christians live a certain life, but the Christian church as a church is called to do something organizationally to change the structure of life in which the church is to find its opportunity to grow. It is my judgment that the greatest debate in the Presbyterian church in our day is the extent to which some will wish the church as a church to act in some fashion upon the state and others will move toward increased personal piety and non-involvement in political matters. Perhaps a basic illustration of this move is in the conflict of recent date where the Amish Dutch (a German tradition group in Iowa) wished to be left to the quiet pursuit of its own way of life, especially the education of their own children.

Paul and Liberty of Conscience

Liberty of conscience is a different kind of problem for the Christian than the problem of Christian liberty, although the two are interlocked. It is a man's personal conscience which leads him eventually to oppose the overrule of an ungodly state. In general, however, the liberty of conscience has to do with a man's moral life, his ethical decisions, his freedom as a Christian, as against his role as citizen.

Here again we swing between two poles, this time represented by law and by grace. This Christian is no longer under law, especially the minutiae of a legal Code, but under grace. And yet Paul says, "For freedom Christ set us free, yet use not that freedom for an occasion to the flesh." There is freedom for the Christian, but the law is "the school teacher toward Christ" and, therefore, has its uses in guidance and discipline, and control.

One of the classic treatments of this problem is found in I Corinthians, chapter 8. The problem for the Christian church was the eating of food offered to idols and after such an offering people might gather around to eat the dedicated food. Or, because the food had been offered to the idol it might be sold in the market place at a cheaper price, and Christians like others would want to buy the bargain meat. The question then was whether the Christians had the right to eat meat that had been used for religious purposes in recognition of an idol. Paul makes it plain that food is food and nothing else, and that the offering of it to an idol makes no difference in its essence. He recognized that many Christians in that day could easily see it for what it was, simply meat. He also recognized that because of the cultural background of those who had come into the Christian church, and because of their early religious habits and training, there might be a real problem posed for some Christians of tender conscience. He thus allowed that from the standpoint of knowledge the Christian could very well know that what he was doing was right, but he was at great pains to point out that what one does with his advanced knowledge may well serve as a stumbling block to one who has not reached that stage in his Christian freedom. What then is the sophisticated Christian, the *knowing* one, to do about his sensitive brother? Well, here is the summation as Paul gives it: "Wherefore, if meat maketh my brother to offend, I will eat no flesh while the world stands, lest I make my brother to offend."

What seems to be at stake here is not a question of my knowledge against my brother's ignorance, but rather a question of my love toward my brother. I am wrong even if right in theory if what I do in my superiority gives my brother the kind of example which makes him override his own conscience in the matter and, therefore, stumble. Unless love dictates my action it is possible that my pride of knowledge in and of itself can be dismally unchristian. I am, therefore, caught in the same kind of bind that we recognize in the church-state problem, the necessity of making a decision in the face of contrary demands.

An idea which has been gaining wider and wider acceptance in the last one hundred years comes under the general name of existentialism. The word itself is impressive and imposing, but is not really difficult to understand. It is an emphasis on the idea of "existence" or the "moment of existence," and what writers have been saying from the time of Kierkegaard to the present (and it has a great vogue in the present) is only this; namely, that it is impossible to write a legal code book covering every single decision in the life of every single man. Laws speak to large issues and great principles, and the individual man must discover what is demanded of him in the light of those laws in the "moment of existence" in which he makes his own ethical decision. To go back to the Corinthian church, it is quite possible that a Christian could eat the meat offered to idols and feel no touch of conscience, but the existential situation might change, and he might there discover himself sitting at meat with a man whose conscience on the matter would change the total *situation*. (Existentialism in ethics is often called *situational* ethics.) What then is the Christian called upon to do? The situation being what it is, for love's sake, that is, for the sake of the good of his brother, he will not eat meat on that particular occasion.

This kind of ethical decision has almost endless possibilities and ramifications. Men in business say that they are called on to make what they call "responsible compromises." A politician may work in the direction of what he calls "the art of the possible." Every person who votes on election day recognizes that it is a Christian's duty to vote yet at the same time that he casts his vote he also recognizes that he is voting between two fallible men and not between right and wrong or light and darkness. Vote he must, but with the recognition that he is, as far as he is able to see, voting in the direction of right but not voting "absolutely right." The situation being what it is, the existential moment in which he finds himself, the situation, dictates what his Christian decision must be. It is possible that a parent will spank a child on one day and not spank a child on another day for the same offense, but he will do so in a judgment based on love for the child and shaped by what the existential situation then requires. I can see, for example, where it might be moral to spank a child who is surrounded by a loving family and not spank a child who is in an orphanage. The situation demands different actions at different moments of existence, but always for Christ's sake.

Paul works over this problem in a variety of ways in I Corinthians, and once again we are not given a clear-cut series of decisions to follow but the same middle ground of decision where law does speak clearly – but so does love.

It is still part of the Calvinistic tradition, however, that the law simply as law has its place. As Paul suggests in Romans, it is the law that gives the consciousness of sin, and it is the consciousness of sin that leads us into the hands of the Saviour. It is our failure over against the law that makes us seek grace and rejoice in the Gospel. It is only the man who has wrestled with the law and discovered his own weakness who finds the need for strength beyond himself.

More than this the law is the framework within which and upon which love may work. Jesus said in the Sermon on the Mount, "I came not to destroy the law and the prophets but to fulfill," to give filling or content to the framework of the law, to give it heart and proper motive. He also said with regard to the law, "Not one jot or one tittle shall pass away until all is fulfilled." Again, the law is not to be dismissed; rather it is to have content and purpose and motive. It is true that the Christian is free, but he is not free to be lawless. Those who cry out against legalism ought to be faced with the question, do you want, then, illegalism? Those who cry out against moralism, do you want, then, immoralism? Whatever we may mean by love as against law, or grace as against law, we cannot mean that we have the right as Christians to do something *less* than the law recognizes or allows. Our freedom is to be something *more* than the law allows.

Paul again in I Corinthians, this time in chapter 6, warns against the Christians going to the law to settle their problems. He recognizes that the Christian like any other citizen has certain legal rights, but he also says (6:17), "Why do ye not rather take wrong? Why do ye not rather suffer yourselves to be defrauded?" The Christian rejoices in the law. He has no notion of doing something less than this, but he can do something more. Having been given his rights under the law he still has the higher privilege of forgiving, of refusing to demand his rights. At the same time there is no place for him to express this grace toward his brother until or unless the law has had its way. It is not a question of law versus grace, but the plain fact that grace cannot operate until the law makes its demands.

There was a couple who finally went to court to break up

their marriage. The husband was able to swear truthfully that he had broken no law toward his wife. He had supported her. He had not abused her. He had been faithful to her. And yet the wife had her case. He had not loved her. This is where we see the relationship of law and love. No man has the right to be lawless, but he has the privilege within the framework of the law to be loving.

We may remember where we discussed earlier what Jonathan Edwards had to say about the freedom of the Christian when he said Christian freedom is actually the freedom to do good and that no one has this freedom, as Edwards would suggest, until he has the newness of life which Christ has given him. There is something of the same sort of teaching here. All kinds of men can keep the law for all kinds of reasons. It is the Christian's privilege to go beyond the keeper of the law not only in his motive but also in high and positive expression beyond anything the law could demand. We have all noticed people who are well-versed in the laws of good manners who can use their very good manners as an expression of cruelty. The heart of good manners is in the heart, and whereas two men might act equally in their good manners, there is all the difference in the world between them because of their regard or disregard of the person toward whom they are expressing these manners.

One time in college we were making preparations for a formal dinner, and we decided to have caviar. None of us had ever eaten caviar, but this was a good way for us to show off to the girls whom we invited to our dinner. The caviar was served on pieces of toast, and the chef had given us the inside word that the toast was to be picked up in our fingers. This was good manners. All of the men knew this, but all of them waited with a suppressed superiority to see what "ladies first" would bring about when the girls were under the necessity to start the meal. We had manners, but we desperately needed real manners. We were using our legal attainments as a cruel opportunity for the expression of our pride. It was small-mindedness in a disgraceful sort of way.

There is a "new morality" abroad today, and it is based on the idea that in any given situation one is directed not by law but by love. Well and good. Augustine was saying the same sort of thing when he said, "Love God and do as you please." Paul was supporting the same viewpoint when he said, "Love is the fulfillment of the law." We can assume for the sake of argument that when a man loves perfectly he will do perfectly but who can say that he loves perfectly? Who can say that he knows enough to know what his own acts will develop in wave after wave of influence from his decision? This is why we still need the control of the law even for the new morality or the new morality can become just a new rationalization for the old immorality.

Until society is perfectly Christian the magistrate must bear the sword. Until a man is perfected in the image of God he is still under the law. Just as the state is the framework under which the church has its opportunity, so the law is the control on a man until his love is made perfect.

CHAPTER 6 – *Questions for Discussion*

1. What is the problem between Christian freedom and the demands of Christian citizenship?
2. Can one who obeys God also obey the State?
3. Is the question of our duty to God and duty to the State ever fully resolved?
4. How does the Christian finally resolve it?
5. Can a Christian ever justify revolution?
6. What is the American solution to the church-state problem?
7. Relate Bible reading in the schools to the church-state problem.
8. What freedom does the Christian have in moral decision with reference to the state law and with reference to the Ten Commandments?
9. Explain the terms "existentialism" and "situational ethics."
10. If love is the only Christian absolute, how does it determine moral decision?

Chapter Seven

THE CHURCH AND THE COMMUNION OF SAINTS

As a starting place we might as well look at two Greek words although this may take a little patience. We all know such words as ecclesiastic and ecclesiastical and we perhaps know the word *ecclesia*. We recognize that all of them refer to the church. These words all come from two Greek words *ek* meaning "out" and *kaleein*, "to call." *Ekkaleein* means "to call out." We have changed the letter "k" to the letter "c" in our language, but the idea is still the same and still clear. The church is basically made up of those who have been "called out," and in Christian circles this means those who have been called out from the world. Because it is a Greek word it also had a Greek usage. For the Greeks it meant some kind of a political group which had been called out of the ordinary affairs of life for some political purpose; and, of course, it was a visible group meeting in a certain place. The church also, therefore, is a group of people called out from the ordinary pursuits of life for the accomplishment of whatever purpose was involved in that call, and it is a visible group meeting in a certain place.

Generally any discussion of the church carries one back to the very beginnings where Abraham was called out from his country and from his father's house in order that God might do something with him and his family. Whatever it was that was to be accomplished in Abraham and his descendants was done in order that Abraham and his descendants might do something for God to the world from which they had been called. God said to Abraham at the time of his call, "Blessing I have blessed you. Be thou a blessing." Those called of God are not only those to whom God does something, but they are those through whom God accomplishes His purposes to the world.

In the case of the descendants of Abraham, those who were called began a kind of theocracy as opposed to a democracy. They were supposed to be directly under the leadership of God as that leadership was experienced through such men as Moses, and there was an identity between the church and the state. The children of Israel, as they were called, having been brought together for God's prupose, found themselves in an organized group in which the lines of the church and the state overlapped. Community and control were supposed to be direct expressions of their total religious life. This is why the book of Leviticus, for example, has in it both ecclesiastical and civil laws, for there was to be no hard and fast line between those two areas of man's life and responsibility. The children of Israel apparently lost their way for two reasons: (1) They tried to identify themselves with the world from which they were supposed to have been called; and (2) they forgot that they were called, not because they were a special breed of some sort, but because God wanted to use them as a channel of His blessing to other men. They became a closed community. It was easy for pride to be one of the marks of the chosen people.

The Nature of the Church

The church in the New Testament is called by Paul the New Israel, and ought to have the same traits that we have suggested in the call to Abraham and his descendants. Those who are in the New Israel are called out of the world or away from the way of the world in order that they might be trained and fitted to help the world. The word disciple is relevant here. A disciple is a learner under a certain discipline and preparation for the sake of service. The word apostle is relevant here. An apostle is one who is particularly called to give the authoritative message of God to the church and through the church to the world.

In the gospels we can observe how the New Israel got underway. John the Baptist had some close followers of his own as he carried on his ministry of preparation. When Jesus appeared on the stage of history, John announced Him in these words, "Behold the Lamb of God that taketh away the sin of the world." This was a statement heavy with theological content and meaning for anyone acquainted with the Jewish religion. John the Baptist was talking about a certain kind of person who was to perform certain redemptive acts, and one who followed this Jesus would have to believe that He was the one chosen of God for man's redemption. We must note at the outset, therefore, that when John's disciples left him to follow Jesus they did so because of a certain content of belief regarding the nature of the One whom they followed and a certain content of belief regarding the nature of His task. Later, when Jesus called the disciples from their fishing or from their other worldly pursuits, such as the tax gathering of Matthew, He called them to a period of training in order that they might be sent out to train others and create a body of believers who would believe as the disciples believed and set before the world the possibility of the acceptance of the truth concerning who Jesus Christ is and what He came to do.

Right here we should note the words of Peter in a crisis situation where many were refusing to follow Christ because of His high claims. "To whom shall we go?" asked Peter, "Thou hast the words of eternal life." What Jesus was and what Jesus taught created the center around which those people gathered. They were called away from loyalty and commitment to anyone else or anything else, and their new life was because their new starting place was centered in the life and teachings of Christ. In the account which we read in the book of Acts where the Holy Spirit came upon the church we see (and we are treating this very briefly) where men were gathered together because of the content of the message of the apostles; and, when the Spirit came upon the church, we must be sure to notice (as it is reported at the end of the second and fourth chapters of Acts) that those who followed Christ were all of one heart and in one place and no one counted anything that he had as his own. They took care of each one according to his need; and, if anyone had anything, he brought it to the disciples' feet to be shared with the others. Those who were "called out" were called into a fellowship which expressed itself in a community, which community was a revelation to the world about it of what men really believed as expressed by what they actually did.

In the church today most of us are aware of the church because it is a certain kind of institution organized into a certain kind of congregation situated in a certain place in the community. Certain things go on in the life of that church which may have to do with worship or teaching and may have to do with some service to society. All such things are true of the church, but we keep forgetting that when a person becomes a member of any church he does so because he has assured someone in the membership (usually an official body) that he also *believes* concerning Jesus Christ what the church claims to be true concerning Jesus Christ.

Entering the Church

The entrance now into the life of the church is as it was in the beginning, an act of belief. Abraham is called "The Father of the Faithful," and we are told that what he believed was "counted to him as righteousness." This is by way of saying that the church had its start and must have its continuity in some body of belief and some statement of faith, some agreement as to what Christianity is all about. This is why churches have confessions and bodies of doctrine; and, I suppose, this is why churches differ from one another, because they insist that certain truths regarding Jesus Christ are more important than other things. They throw their weight of emphasis in certain areas of truth and may even deny that what one group of people thinks is important is really of any importance at all. And so the Church of Jesus Christ becomes the churches of Jesus Christ, and one of the great moves in the history of the church today is the attempt to discover a body of belief around which all the churches can adhere. At the same time, one of the dangers of this movement toward unity is that the body of belief may be minimized for the sake of getting churches together. It seems impossible in the very nature of the case that the church can have any reality at all divorced from a plain doctrinal position. This may sound to some as leading to intolerance, and this may well be true. Whether such intolerance is a bad thing or not is worth our attention.

Let us remind ourselves that when the first disciples believed certain things about Jesus they gave up whatever it was they were doing to commit their life entirely to His calling and His discipline. It is difficult to see how a man can commit his whole life to something he really doesn't believe in, and the other side of this is that if a man really does believe in something it is virtually impossible for him not to commit his life to it. If he says that a certain truth doesn't matter, it is unlikely that he believes that it is really the truth. If he holds that one truth is equal to another truth, he hasn't thought very seriously about truth itself. What I am trying to say is this: a thing is true or it is not; and if it is true, we can hardly say first that it doesn't matter; or second, that it can be treated like half-truth.

It may be that we try to center our lives around too many statements of truth which often we haven't thought through, but it bears repeating that a man cannot commit himself really to something he doesn't hold to be true; and that, if he does really hold it to be true, he finds himself called to commit himself at that very point. This kind of commitment to truth might empty our churches, but it would make a reality of the churches that remained. Instead of a great many people around the edges being unconvinced or partially so, we would find ourselves with a hard knot of committed people. So much of our urging toward the giving of our gifts or the involvement in service would be totally unnecessary because no one would "belong" to church unless he really believed that the thing to which he belonged was absolutely true and therefore demanded his full commitment.

It is here, I suppose, that we move over into what we call the communion of the saints. A body of people who are gathered together around a core of belief and commitment already have communion. They have a oneness of spirit in their oneness of loyalty. In my judgment communion and fellowship are not things that can be whipped up or organized into being. A real communion is a living product of people who are already united in what they believe and are already committed to it. They are in the nature of the case "together" because their belief and loyalty necessarily put them together.

For many years on a college campus as a dean of men I was well aware of all the activities in which the men were involved, and it was interesting to see certain activities come and go in the life of the college. To take as an easy example, I remember a group of chess players organizing a chess club. There weren't a great many of them, and they knew by the nature of their interest that not everyone on the campus could be enlisted, but they themselves were interested enough in chess to spend time on the game and the study of the game and a sharing of the problems of chess with like-minded students on other campuses. What did they do with their time when they had time? They played chess. Where did they go when they followed their natural inclinations? They went to their chess group. As I observed them, I appreciated (and not because I was a chess player) how their involvement in this one loyalty involved them with one another and bound them together.

But after a while there were not enough chess players on the campus to make out of the group a going concern. And so they tried to hold the group together without the kind of interest that created the group in the first place. Each president of the group in turn was determined that the "organization" must not fall apart under his presidency, and so there were membership drives which succeeded in getting members but not chess players. And this is really what finally topped everything. The first thing I knew I saw where the chess group for one of their meetings was announcing an outside speaker! The fire had gone out.

For chess club read any other organization in which you have membership, and see where you stand in the story of this particular group. More seriously consider the experience of that chess club as an epitome of the church, and where your church stands. We have to pay for our buildings. We can't stand the idea that the "organization" can fail in our time and so we are constantly tempted to keep the thing going, and pretty soon we can have scores of people in any one congregation who have no notion of what it is all about and no sense of commitment. Their membership is incidental and coincidental. It can end up with the giving of a pittance in money or time or it may be marked by nothing better than "going to church."

What is even worse is that such members will flock out to church on those days when there is a "communion service" as if there were some special merit in that. There will be "fellowship" dinners and all kinds of attempts to sell "togetherness" and pretty soon those most loyal to the group will discover that their time is spent in duties and routines of increasing vacuousness. The church in such a condition (probably more success-minded than it should be) is trying to solve its problems from the wrong end. They think that communion is something they must create or bring to pass. It is quite impossible. Communion is a product produced by any body of people who believe something fully and are committed to it. In that commitment their communion arrives.

Martin Luther

When Luther broke away from the church of Rome, or more exactly was forced out of the church of Rome, he knew as well as anyone knows that a man cannot be a Christian by himself. "No man is an island." All he could do, therefore, was to hold to supreme loyalty to Christ and urge others to find his direction as access to their Saviour. When they did and insofar as they did, they found themselves together with Luther. Men and women cannot be "in Christ" and not be together because in this basic relationship they have the ground for their relationship to one another. It is amazing how people find each other because of their interests, and thus people who find Christ and His call the supreme interest never fail to find one another. What clouds the issue is that so many people without this basic commitment have become a part of the physical manifestation of what we call the church and are in no way a part of the reality, only a part of its facade.

Luther and Calvin and the other reformers in speaking of the church understood the meaning of the church visible and the church invisible. The Westminster divines who laid down the doctrinal bases for Presbyterianism as we know it today also understood this difference. What we have to understand is the visible church and the invisible church, but we must also understand that the invisible church must in some way express itself visibly.

Let us assume for the sake of illustration that a group of people have found each other in Christ and in their commitment to Him (like the chess players); they will normally and naturally *want* to be together; and they will want to do things together for their common calling will urge them to a common expression of their calling. For preparation time or for learning or for their common worship they will have to gather together at stated times at stated places. In the earliest church they met in homes. They could still do the same and some highly committed groups in our day do unite in "house" churches. The point is that however highly spiritual their relationship to God and to each other may be, men are physical creatures as well as spiritual ones; and, therefore they have physical demands. Meeting at specified times and at specified places means that someone therefore must run some kind of an organization for the care of the building, the announcement of times, heating, lighting, all the ordinary physical requirements for the getting together of a group of people.

If such a group has a mission to the world outside of the group, there will have to be money and someone to keep the money and a program and times and places where the program will be brought to bear upon the world. Since the commission of the church is to the whole world there must also be a world mission program; and, as this group gathers with other groups, the plain necessities of distance and travel will require other places of meeting, finances, again program and perhaps eventually someone who arranges for the travel of missionaries "into all the world."

What I am suggesting here is that it is quite impossible for a group, however purified and however spiritual, to rid itself of visibility. I have heard pastors complain that they spend as much as 60 per cent of their time in administration. This may be a high cost and perhaps higher than it needs to be, but we are utterly naive if we think that any group of people, however spiritually motivated, can be free of the routines of organization and administration. As the Westminster divines point out, the invisible church is made up of believers everywhere known only to God, and it is to be expected that many members of many visible churches are not truly believers and, therefore, are not true members of Christ. But the solution of the fact is not to disorganize the church because the true believers are known only to God. True believers as such will of necessity find each other and will of necessity organize for the work of the Gospel, and in the nature of the case will gather around them many who are not true believers. It does a church no good finally to break off from some other church in order to get rid of the overpowering necessities of organization. The organization will come into being almost immediately as soon as such a group of people gets underway in their own special calling.

The True Church

The other side of the picture is this. When we glory in the fact of the visible church — cathedrals, mass meetings, summer camps, colleges, hospitals, works of art, and the like — we have to keep reminding ourselves that whatever the successful church may have in such visible manifestations, the true life of the church and the true membership of the church are not to be confused with the external trappings, even though most of them arose at some time or other as a necessary expression of the true church. The invisible church must express itself visibly, but we make a mistake when we read this backwards and thereby believe that the visible church is the true church. This understanding can save us some heartbreak when we are distressed with some of the ways in which the visible church operates or fails to operate. The true life of the church has not been snuffed out just because at different times and at different places the visible church may have wandered so far away from what we think was true of the simple Galilean. The life goes on, known only to God, nurtured by His Spirit. Those who truly believe express themselves, depending on how the machinery permits, as the Body of Christ at work in the world.

This is a good place to comment on the ecumenical movement in our day. Much has been said and ought to be said about this "scandal" of our church divisions. We need to remind ourselves, however, that there are many divisions inside Roman Catholicism, but their divisions are held together because of the structure of their church with loyalty centered around the Pope and Rome. Thus the divisions do not break out of the organized structure of the church. Differences are settled internally and allowances are made for any particular group with some special concern to organize in a monastery or a teaching brotherhood or some special training school or the like. Divisions in Protestantism, however, because of differences in emphasis, or where the weight is thrown in doctrinal loyalty, result in the appearance of new churches and new denominations. Thus in Protestantism there are more than 200 different groupings although, as is so frequently pointed out, the great divisions of Protestantism probably exist in about seven or eight great organized denominations.

It has always been accepted by the Protestant churches that there are true believers throughout Protestantism and also in Catholicism. This is the belief Protestants hold in the invisible church. The believers finally are known only to God and are known wherever they are in whatever organized church by their loyalty and commitment which only God can judge.

Keeping in mind, however, that what is invisible must express itself visibly one must recognize that the divisions in Protestantism are an expression somehow of a division in spirit and attitude even among the true believers. Although it is not an exact equation, organized division is indicative of division in personal beliefs.

The problem in the ecumenical movement, therefore, is twofold. In the first place, there must be greater concern for teaching, training, doctrinal understanding, and unity of commitment. In the second place, we must be wary about putting churches together organizationally believing by such activity that the churches will really be together or that the members of the churches shall have that unity of spirit apart from which there is no communion at all. We can understand the ecumenical movement in our day if we watch both of these areas of concern.

The so-called fundamentalists or the so-called sectarians are those who hold fast to the idea that nothing really happens apart from sound belief and that any unity apart from true believing is false at the outset. Others holding to the control principle believe that once we are brought together organizationally then in the larger organization a common front can be turned to the outside world in either challenge or service, and that meanwhile inside the organizational structure, work can proceed toward common belief and commitment.

Although this age is marked by the ecumenical movement and although most people believe (especially the church leadership) that we are moving into a day of greater unity, it is not hard to observe that there is also increasing disunity, not because men are divisive in spirit, but because they are deeply concerned about the truth as it is found in Christ. It is almost a tragedy of our day that these two kinds of thinking as they represent, I believe, two kinds of minds, represent a real cleavage in the church perhaps deeper than what we like to call the "scandal" of our denominational divisions. As Troeltsch once observed, there is a church type and a sect type. Both approaches are clearly at work in our day. I can only suppose that as they bear fruit we shall find new alignments and new loyalties. No Christian can be happy over the division of the churches. This is the truth of the ecumenical movement. No Christian can be happy if doctrinal truth is lost by default just to satisfy the drive for unity. This becomes the thrust of the fundamentalist or sectarian groups. On these matters the church is a long way from a satisfactory or a happy solution.

Another problem or series of problems very much to the fore is related to the social action of the church. As we saw in the church described in the book of Acts, the very first move of the early church, based on communion and fellowship, was the creation of some kind of community in which people shared what they had and supported people according to their needs. The church has always supported this drive toward community as necessary to her nature. Israel was to bless all men. The New Israel is to bless all men. The church is the body of Christ at work in the world, and this work can find a multitude of outlets. There was a time when we talked about the personal gospel and the social gospel, but we know better now. There is only one Gospel. The good news is that a man is saved by the grace of God when God accepts him as he is: "In that while we were yet sinners, Christ died for us." But the man who finds himself in this new relationship to God and has the good news of his release from sin and the power of sin, must by his very nature, his new nature, serve God with the whole of his life, and he can serve God only in his service to men.

What is true of one man is true of a group of men; and is, therefore, true of an organized church. It is impossible in the nature of the case for the church to look after only its own well-being and forget the needs of those around it. This is where the Israelites lost their way when they thought of themselves in the wrong way as "God's chosen people." It can also be true of the "elect" (and this is a strong Presbyterian idea) that they think of themselves as God's chosen people and that because they are called out of the world they are, therefore, something special in and of themselves. Not so. The whole idea of election from the beginning of the Bible is "election to service." We are chosen to do something.

A man is put on a team because the people who choose him expect him to play the game. So it is with the members of the church. So it is with the church. They have been made up into the body of Christ and the members of that body all have their own functions, not only toward the care of the body, but toward the activity of the body toward others. From the time of Calvin to the present day it has been a mark of the Presbyterian tradition in social service (as we noted formerly in affairs of state) that the church is to discover the ways and means by which a needy world can be served. One emphasis, of course, is to give to needy men everywhere the good news of the Gospel and this is the program of evangelism, but the church has been touched by the need for doctors and hospitals and orphanages and colleges. Where the debate rages today, and particularly in the Presbyterian family of churches, is whether this social conscience of a church demands the action of the church as an organization.

If the church should speak out on liquor or prostitution, surely live social problems in our day, is there any reason why the church should not also speak out and take a stand and enter into the arena in race, poverty, war, unemployment, housing, and leisure time? Some will argue that it has been the nature of the Presbyterian church to change men who according to their gifts will then change society. Others have argued that it is not enough to preach the Gospel unless we enter into some organization that will give men peace and food so that they may listen to the Gospel. There is no livelier discord in the Presbyterian church than at this very point in this very hour.

To what extent should the church as the church enter actively into politics and social action? Here again we remind ourselves that there is no such thing as a non-social Christian or a non-social church. Perhaps the solution lies not in whether the church should get into the arena of men's social struggles but rather whether the church as a church is rightly organized and structured so to enter in. If, for example, the problem of war or the pursuit of a particular war divides men into political parties (an issue between Goldwater and Johnson for example), can the church hold within her own membership men and women who take diverse views in the political arena when the church as a church enters in on one side or another of the political question? Does the church know enough or can the church know enough to make decisions regarding a specific war which decisions are dividing men in the top echelons of our government who have access to information which the church could not possibly have?

And the further question is, can the church as such, by entering into one side or another of such a problem, negate the burden of her message or destroy her opportunity to bind up the wounds when the conflict is over? Suffice it to say that as far as Presbyterian belief is concerned, there is harsh division in this very day. Yet somehow in terms of her great tradition, the Presbyterian church must discover how to throw herself into some of the great social struggles.

CHAPTER 7 – *Questions for Discussion*

1. What does the term "church" really mean?
2. When and how did the church begin?
3. How is the church related to the confession of certain Christian truths?
4. Should a church begin with a "confession" or with an organization?
5. Distinguish between the invisible and the visible church.
6. If the invisible church is a reality, why must we have a visible church?
7. What do the divisions of the churches say about our oneness in Christ?
8. Will organizational unity give oneness to the church?
9. Do you think the church should engage in social action as an organization or through individuals?
10. If the church takes a stand on a social issue like liquor, should it also take a stand on a social issue like poverty?

Chapter Eight

THE SACRAMENTS: BAPTISM AND THE LORD'S SUPPER

When you stop to think about it, the sacraments of the church are very strange things. Imagine, if you will, what reaction a person might have who has never seen a sacrament, let alone participated in one. What could he possibly think of such goings on in a congregation of mature people performing such strange acts? At a church of Baptists he would see both the minister and the person to be baptized descend into a tank of water, and with the pronouncement of certain words the person to be baptized would be put completely under the water, and this would be something in which the congregation would join in some expression of rejoicing. In some other church he might see an infant in the arms of his father or perhaps in the arms of the minister having water sprinkled on his head with the pronouncement of certain words. In an orthodox church he would see the infant submerged three times in the water of the baptismal fount.

If he were to observe the Lord's Supper, he might see worshipers kneeling at the communion table or at the communion rail receiving a wafer from the hands of a priest, or he would see them receiving a wafer which had been dipped in wine, or he would see the participants taking a small piece of bread and a little sip of wine. In less "sacramental" churches he would see small bits of bread passed out to the members of the congregation after which each member would receive a small glass of wine.

A little boy once asked by his grandmother what went on in the church service reported, "They had some bread and then they drank some grape juice and then everybody had a headache." This was his way of describing the way in which the members of the congregation engaged in silent prayer after "receiving" communion.

The sacraments are strange activities apart from this naive observation for two other reasons. (1) So little relatively of the total of Scripture is given over to the sacraments in the first place, yet they have come to have a quite central place in the life of the church. (2) Whereas the sacraments are supposed to mark initiation into and nurture in the life of the church, and are supposed to unite worshipers in a "communion," the sacraments have, nevertheless, been the means of some of the greatest divisions in the life of thc church. Indeed one of the great divisions, the one between Roman Catholicism and Protestantism, arises over how many sacraments there are and what rites of the church are to be considered sacramental. Our purpose therefore is to come at the sacraments from the Presbyterian viewpoint; and, perhaps in doing so we shall find occasion to explain in some measure what meanings attach to these questions which naturally arise around them.

Protestantism's Two Sacraments

All Protestants, and this includes Presbyterians, have constantly held to two sacraments as against seven held by the Romans Catholics. The seven sacraments of the Roman Catholic Church are baptism, confirmation, matrimony, penance, the Lord's Supper (Eucharist, thanksgiving), holy orders, and extreme unction. Rome has thus made provision at almost every point in a man's life for some sacrament. Baptism is for infants as they become part of the church. Confirmation allows for the child at the age of reason to confirm what was done for him in baptism. Matrimony, as the word suggests, is an attempt to make a sacrament out of marriage. Penance makes provision in both act and word for something to be done about a man's sins. Communion is the feeding on the broken body and the shed blood of Christ for one's nurture in the life of the church. Holy orders is a sacrament by which a man or woman is set aside for a religious vocation. Extreme unction is an action by which at the point of a man's death a covering is made for his sins up to that moment.

Protestantism allows for the importance of these rites and in some fashion makes provision for such things as confirmation, marriage, penance, holy orders (usually called ordination among Protestants) and extreme unction at which time the pastor attempts to establish the faith of a dying person by promises from Scripture. With such importance placed on such rites the natural question then is, why Protestants do not have seven sacraments. The difference lies in an attitude toward truth which also divides Protestantism from Catholicism. Roman Catholics believe that what is established in the practice of the church can be established by tradition as well as by Scripture, whereas Protestants hold to the definitive authority of the Scriptures.

Basing their position, therefore, on the Scriptures, Protestants hold that those rites are sacramental which have two qualities: (1) establishment by Christ, and (2) availability to all people whatever their age or occupation and whether men or women. We can see this difference immediately in something like marriage. Here is a rite of the church which is, of course, available only to people who get married. The same would be true of holy orders which would be a blessing of God only on those who go into holy vocation. These two rites quite evidently, therefore, carry certain graces which are not available to all. It is also evident that such a rite as confirmation or extreme unction was not in any way established by Christ, but became a practice of the church and was eventually hardened into official doctrine. However we might argue the merits of the two positions – two against seven sacraments – this is at least how the differences arose and how they now stand.

Another question is that of what is supposed to take place during a sacrament. Since we are limiting ourselves now to the Presbyterian viewpoint (the viewpoint generally held by all Protestants) we shall do our explaining on that basis. The sacrament has in it certain visible signs or symbols. There is the water of baptism, the bread and wine of communion. Water has always been thought of as useful in initiatory rites and was used by the Israelites in such fashion as reflected in the Old Testament. Water also has a natural symbolism having to do with cleansing. It is, therefore, an apt "sign" for what is supposed to take place. In the communion also it is easy to see with immediacy that the bread and the cup symbolize food and drink, and it so happens that the unleavened bread and the wine were basic in the diet of those who initiated the first Lord's Supper or communion. From that day forward bread and wine, food and drink, have been clear symbols of the idea of nurture. Since the Christian, as we shall try to determine later, is to "feed on" what has been done for him in Christ's redemptive action on the cross, the broken bread and the wine easily symbolize the broken body and shed blood of Jesus Christ.

This is a good place to think a little about symbols. Symbols are what they are in themselves but they also convey something more than themselves. Take for example the words which we write or the words with which we communicate our thoughts and speech. These are symbols which are acceptable to anyone who happens to know the language, and it is significant that once we have learned the language we really bypass the words since we are concerned primarily with the thought that they convey. Once we master the symbols we can receive with the same immediacy the thoughts. We are not to stop with the symbols. They simply communicate. The message of salvation is preached and taught, and by this means we receive and know and, it is hoped, experience the truth. In a simple fashion, then, the symbols of both baptism and the Lord's Supper are conveyors for truth and experience. Someone has called them "visible words," and it was John Calvin who insisted that in every church service the Gospel ought to be preached in words and set forth visibly in sacraments. Although he never was able to accomplish this in the Geneva church he nevertheless, by his urging of this, made clear what he thought the sacraments were to do, i.e., they were to present visibly the same Gospel which was heard audibly.

Sacrament Defined

One definition of a sacrament is "the visible sign of an invisible reality." Or again, "the physical sign of a spiritual reality." This is not as difficult as it may sound if we think in terms of other symbols. Anyone can argue that an American flag is made out of nothing but material, and it is easy to place a monetary value on the material. The goods in the flag may be valued at $3.50 or $25.98; and, if one wants to be literal about it, it is impossible to prove that the material in the flag is worth anything more. This being so, a man can purchase the flag at the price asked (I suppose all flags are some time or another purchased), and then feel that he can do with the flag as he pleases because he owns it. And yet in a sense he cannot. What would happen to a man who bought an American flag, paid the full price and therefore owned it, who would then walk out into the street and shred it or trample it in the dirt? Even those people who most insist that a flag is nothing but material would probably trample that man because they would insist that even though he owned it in one way he did not own it in another.

The flag contains or "communicates" all kinds of realities and values beyond the price of the flag or his ownership of it. It is not only the kind of symbolism where we say that the red stands for courage, and the white stands for purity, and the blue stands for loyalty, and the stars stand for the states, and the stripes stand for the original colonies; but there is a "real" content in the flag with a certain spiritual quality to it. Indeed there is a kind of equation so that what you do to the flag when you honor it, or what you do to the flag when you disgrace it, you do to that spiritual content. Therefore you are judged by how you act or react toward that physical sign. Who gave the flag this content? Somewhere, somehow it became an *official sign* of everything that means so much to one who calls himself an American.

So with the sacraments. A physical sign was given an *official* meaning, and from that point on, once the signs have been set aside for holy purposes (and the word "holy" means set aside) the sign becomes a different sort of thing because of what it contains and what it communicates. There is now a physical sign of a spiritual content.

Baptism

We turn now to a specific consideration of the sacrament of baptism. The Roman Catholic church and a great many Protestants believe in infant baptism (sometimes called paedo-baptism) and in general the same practice is followed. The parents present the child for baptism, and the priest or minister holding some water on the head of the child pronounces the words of baptism. This is done after certain vows have been taken by the parents on behalf of the child, and these vows have to do with the instruction and training of the child in the things of Christ. In the Orthodox churches there is also the practice of infant baptism except that the priest immerses the child three times in the name of the Father and the Son and the Holy Spirit.

The chief division in Protestantism is represented by the Baptist churches and some groups of churches called generally the Christian churches. Baptism for them is reserved for adults and the practice is immersion. The reasoning of the Baptists and likeminded Protestants is that baptism is a sacrament of cleansing and can be performed only on those who have reached the age of discretion and who, therefore, are conscious of their sin and their need of repentance. It is impossible in this viewpoint to see how any infant can be thought of as responsible or knowledgeable, and therefore, the cleansing is impossible apart from the baptized person accepting his condition and his need for cleansing. The reasoning behind immersion is that since the whole person is to be cleansed and, therefore saved, the whole person should be immersed in the waters of baptism as a sign and symbol of the fact.

Two problems are built into this Baptist position on baptism. The first problem arises over what might be called the age of discretion. It is not only a question of when a child becomes an adult, but more exactly of when a child has reached an age when he is able to make some kind of decision regarding his sin and his need of a Saviour. It is significant that the age at which this can be done has become increasingly depressed in the recent history of the Baptists. The other problem is whether the supervising minister can baptize a young person or an adult on the basis of anything stronger than the *assumption* that the person is truly repentant and truly accepts what is being done for him in Christ's name. We must keep reminding ourselves that when a person is baptized or when a person joins the church the actions of the officials can be based only on presumptive evidence. Protestants other than Baptists argue this way. Since baptism is on the basis of presumptive evidence should baptism rest more on the basis of public confession by the person baptized or on the promises of God revealed in Scripture which are "for you and for your children"? This is really the turn. Is what happens in baptism something that depends on man's statement of what has happened to him or on God's promise of what He will do? We cannot turn aside here to pursue this discussion, but I think it clearly turns on this question.

The churches which practice infant baptism take their starting place from the initiatory rite of the Israelites; namely, circumcision. Volumes have been written on this strange practice which in ancient times and in a wide variety of tribal practices even in our own day, sometimes did and sometimes did not contain some particular religious significance. In general, circumcision has always been an initiatory rite; and, as is so often true in both Old Testament and New Testament religion, some practices common among men were given new meaning or content. This is what seems to have happened with circumcision which was widely practiced before the days of Abraham and was used in a wide variety of ways apart from the Israelites.

What is significant, it must be constantly borne in mind, in the Israelite's practice, is that for Abraham, the Father of the Faith, circumcision followed immediately on his confession of faith. He was an adult and he had made an adult decision, but what was peculiar about it was that from that point onward even though circumcision was a sign of faith it was practiced with boys eight days old. The question which the modern Baptist puts to others as to how baptism can be a sign of faith or of cleansing in one who cannot make an adult decision is immediately aggravated by observing that this first sign of faith among the Israelites was used on eight-day-old boys who evidently could not possibly make any decision.

Baptism and Circumcision

During the history of the Israelites circumcision came to have an increasingly spiritual emphasis. It was the peculiar requirement that their hearts should be circumcised. It was the cry of the prophets to the Jews later that Israelites could be raised up from the stones themselves if one were talking only of national identity and the sign of circumcision which accompanied it. The whole point of circumcision, insisted on over and over again, was that it was the sign truly of a spiritual content; and, while this spiritual insistence was being made, circumcision was still being practiced on eight-day-old boys. It seems possible, therefore, that the sign of salvation by faith beginning with Abraham, the Father of the Faith, carried its content not only on adult believers, but on to their children.

The New Testament parallel for circumcision is baptism as the Lord's Supper is for the Passover. Baptism is also the sign of those who belong to the household of faith. "The promises are to you and to your children." And the sign that the child is a child of promise is the sign of baptism. It is quite possible, as Baptists point out, that a child so baptized might well grow up with no spiritual interest or loyalty whatsoever. Does this mean that what happened at baptism accomplished nothing? I think so. Protestants generally do not hold to baptismal regeneration. That is, the baptism does not accomplish salvation. This is the kind of superstition which people might have who are fearful that a child might die unbaptized. The sign signifies that the child is a member of the household of faith by virtue of the promises made to the parents and in the sacramental vows which the parents for their children have promised to fulfill. It is because the parental vows are faithfully carried out that baptism may have its effect.

The clearest illustration that I can think of takes me back to the abdication of Edward the Eighth when he gave up his throne for Wallis Warfield Simpson. When Edward was born, the guns were fired on the occasion of his birth because the heir apparent was now on the scene. As the heir apparent, he immediately inherited all the gifts due him as a member of the royal family. If both his parents had died on the day of his birth, he would still have had these privileges of rank and gifts of money and land, rightfully his by virtue of his birth. And until he did grow to maturity to take over consciously what already belonged to him unconsciously, a regent would have been set up to rule *for* him until he could rule for himself. We must make the point very clear. What he had in his infancy had nothing to do with any decision he made as an infant. As we pursue the story, however, we find him trained for kingship because of his royalty. But we also discover that in his days of discretion he first of all treated lightly the responsibilities which came along with the gifts, and in a moment of great decision he determined to give up the gifts because he no longer wished to carry the responsibility.

This is what happens in infant baptism. Surely there is some kind of a difference in a child by virtue of the fact that his parents are children of God, and we must assume here the truth of that relationship of the parents. The vows of the parents are that they shall bring up this child as an inheritor of the gifts of promise. They may well do so with all sincerity and still fail. The point is that the child has these gifts by virtue of his relationship until he wishes to make a decision as to whether he shall accept the responsibilities of a Christian life which are the other side of the coin when we talk about Christian gifts. For the Baptist who insists on adult baptism, we can only point out that with some frequency also there are adults who are "saved" who with the passing of the years forget the mature adult decision which they made and no longer think of themselves as children of God.

The Lord's Supper

With regard to the Lord's Supper there have also been some divisions, and I think we can organize them into four distinctions. The Roman Catholic Church has held to what is called transubstantiation. They believe in what they call "the miracle of the mass," that the actual "substance" of the body and blood of Christ goes over (itself) and becomes the "substance" of the bread and wine. This is based on a view of matter which was strongly held in mediaeval times and has been given serious consideration by philosophers in every generation. Material things they say have "accidents" and "substance." Take, for example, the table in the room in front of you. The "accidents" of that table are those things which touch the sense. The table has a certain color and size, a certain texture, and, I suppose, even a certain taste. These are "accidental" qualities which could vary with all the tables in the world while you still talk about the concept or the idea of a table. The table is the substance of its many appearances and accidents. We never get into the "thing itself" by way of our senses.

So it was with the body of Christ. Multitudes experienced Him through their senses "in the flesh," but the real Christ was known beyond these appearances. This was His "substance." In "the miracle of the mass" it is this substance which now goes over and becomes the substance of the bread and the wine. He is, therefore, physically present although hidden under the "accidents." Roman Catholics base this on a serious consideration of Christ's words at the first Lord's Supper, "This *is* my body. This *is* my blood." They have tried to figure out a way to hold to the literality of the text and still allow that according to our *senses* no such change takes place in the wafer or the wine. One could point out that if they wish to be so literal they might have a real problem where the words of Scripture tell us that we are to "drink the *cup*." The necessity for a figure of speech here is immediately evident.

Luther tried to hold to the literal words, "This is my body," but could not make an equation between the substance of the bread and the substance of Christ because he thought this was idolatry, a kind of worship of things. The Lutherans came up with the word consubstantiation meaning that the substance of Christ is truly present "in, around and under" the bread. This is pretty hard to grasp; but what Luther had in mind, apparently, was that we cannot equate the bread with Christ's body, but Scripture insists that He is present.

How is He present? Well, in the same way that heat has its presence in a piece of iron that has been made red hot. We do not confuse the iron and the heat. Nevertheless, the heat is "in, around and under" the iron, and it is impossible to touch the iron at any point without at the same time touching the heat. The two are not the same thing or the same sort of thing. Nevertheless, they are completely united, so that when we take one we take the other. So in the Lord's Supper: Christ's body is truly in the bread but not the same as the bread. Yet when we take the bread we take Him.

Zwingli, the Swiss reformer, took the view which I expect most Protestants hold if they think about this at all; namely, that the manner of Christ's presence is a mystery which we make a mistake in trying to analyze, and that the important thing in the Lord's Supper is the act of remembrance. He threw his emphasis not on the words, "This is my body," but on the words, "This do in remembrance of me."

John Calvin, and therefore the Calvinists and in tradition the Presbyterians, have held to what is called the *real presence* theory. Christ is *really* present but not *physically* present. This theory was back of what we said originally about the symbol of the American flag. One is trained to appreciate a symbol and to find in it content beyond its superficial appearance, but the content is a spiritual reality and not physical or substantial as both the Roman Catholics or Lutherans would argue. Calvin used an illustration of a tear on the face of a child. One observing this tear could say, "This is sadness." Would this mean that if we could catch those tears in a vial and save them up we could then open up the vial any time we wish and take out several drops of sadness? This is ridiculous on the face of it as we know. Nevertheless, when we see the tears on the face of a child, we say, "This is sadness." What we mean is that the physical signs are directly related to the inner experience of the child so that when we see the signs we recognize the reality, but the reality is in the mind and heart of the child, a spiritual reality of which the tears are signs.

We use the same kind of language when we try to give someone directions on a map. We say, "This is New York and this is Chicago and this is Route 20 running from New York to Chicago." No one really believes that the marks on a map are in any way the two cities nor the highway, but unless a person accepts the symbolism it is pretty hard to direct him on his trip; and, of course, we all know that the trip is of infinitely greater importance than the map. The only thing is, you can hardly enjoy the trip unless you accept the map. The symbols of the map are the way in to the experience or, if you like, they are the conveyances by which the experience is made possible.

No one goes to the theater unless he is willing to accept what the program says, "This is the living room at three o'clock in the afternoon on Monday," and in the last act, "This is the living room three days later." We cannot get what the play has to say unless we accept the symbols. This is why in much modern drama some of the symbolism is made starkly simple because the dramatists know that the observer of the dramatic experience must accept "by faith" the means by which the experience is conveyed.

There is sense, therefore, in what Presbyterians are saying when they talk about the *real* presence. They go on to say that one receives the presence only through faith. Christ initiated the Lord's Supper and commanded that we should do this in remembrance of Him, and surrounded the sacrament with certain assurances of His presence. As the reformers pointed out, if a mouse should come in and eat some of the bread of the sacrament which had been blessed, it would be a very strange thing to consider what had happened to the literal body of Christ. The Presbyterian answer to this is that the sign and symbol mean nothing until they are received by faith on the part of the communicant just as surely as the items on a stage mean nothing without the willingness of the observer to accept their content.

The question is frequently raised as to the necessity of the sacrament of the Lord's Supper. If Christians believe Christ is always present, why do we need this sign and symbol? We must point out, therefore, that what happens in the Lord's Supper is not a difference in kind in regard to Christ's presence but a difference in intensity. Since we are not purely spiritual beings but also physical beings, we are under the necessity of the physical for the conveyance of spiritual realities. We are surrounded by sunshine on a sunny day for example, but a reading glass can pull together all the rays of the sunshine with such intensity that flame can be induced under the glass. What surrounded us in general now in intensity makes something light up.

Perhaps an engagement ring is the finest illustration of this, or a wedding ring if you like. The young woman may be surrounded by love and generally conscious of that love every hour of the day; but, when she looks at her ring, the bride-to-be is made sharply conscious "in remembrance" of all sorts of things regarding this love. A person does not have to say to another person, "I love you," but such words and likewise gifts and remembrances and remembered days such as birthdays and wedding anniversaries, bring "remembrance" and one is strengthened and, indeed, delighted by what takes place in the act of remembrance which is brought into intensity by the sign and the symbol.

A young man going into the military was offered a blank check or any other gift by his father. The father wanted so much to go with the son and support him in any way he could. The father had a habit of twirling a pocket knife on the end of his watch chain and interestingly enough, the boy asked for that knife. Wherever he went after that he carried his father's knife, and in time of fear, or loneliness, or temptation he could take out the knife and manipulate it as his father habitually did; and all the good things of his family would come flooding in to support him. So it was in the words of Jesus. This do "in remembrance of me." The signs and symbols make real the experience of the promise, "Lo, I am with you always even unto the end."

CHAPTER 8 – *Questions for Discussion*

1. Why are the sacraments considered so important?
2. Why do Protestants hold to two sacraments while the Roman Catholics hold to seven?
3. What are the Protestant sacraments, and what are the Catholic sacraments?
4. The sacraments are called "the visible signs of invisible reality." Explain.
5. Why do many churches believe that infant baptism is valid?
6. Why are baptism and circumcision considered together?
7. What views are taken on the Lord's Supper by the Roman Catholics, the Lutherans, and the Calvinists?
8. What is the difference between the physical presence and the real presence of Christ in the Lord's Supper?
9. If Christ is always present with the believer, why do we need the sacrament at all?

Chapter Nine

CHURCH GOVERNMENT

It is out of church government that the name Presbyterian arises, for the Presbyterian system of government is based upon what is called a presbytery; and a Presbyterian church, however carefully or closely it may hew to the line of doctrine, is always marked by this governmental structure.

The operating unit is the congregation, and a number of congregations in a geographical area are organized into what is called a presbytery. In a larger geographical area the presbyteries are gathered together in synods (these normally cover one of the states in the continental United States), and synods and presbyteries eventually head up in what is called the General Assembly. The General Assembly because of its character as a national meeting and because of the accompanying publicity which these great meetings have gives the impression that it is the ruling body of the Presbyterian church but this is not so. Actions taken at the General Assembly level have to be voted on by the presbyteries. The presbytery is the unit which finally controls both theology and active policy.

It is also generally believed that the local congregation, because of its locale and its building and its organization, actually controls the life of that congregation. Frequently this is so, but in terms of final control, presbytery again is the ruling body. This frequently comes as a shock to members of the congregation when they discover that in spite of the gifts which they have given to the congregation even the ownership of the church rests in the presbytery. Also, in spite of the fact that they call their own minister and pay his salary and provide his housing, the minister is actually a member of presbytery and not a member of his own congregation, and it is impossible for the congregation to hire or fire their own minister without the agreement of presbytery.

The Presbyterian Form of Government

The whole Presbyterian system is a representative system. We think of our own national government as being a democracy, and at some stages in its history and in some small villages and towns it is still possible to think of the whole citizenship gathering to act on public matters. As a matter of fact, however, our national structure is not a democracy but a republic. What is done is done by representatives, and some kind of a balance has been reached by having representation for states and representation for population groups. The Presbyterian system is also a republic in that it rests not on the pure democracy of the local congregation, but on representatives which are sent to presbytery and in turn to synods and to the General Assembly. It does not even follow that the representatives of a congregation meeting in presbytery or in the higher courts of the church necessarily vote according to the wishes of the congregation at these higher church meetings where they "represent" their congregations, but they must vote frequently according to the discussion and debate which they hear and in which they specifically participate.

Representatives, of course, as is also true in civil affairs, shall want to represent the group from which they come; but they are not under the control of that group that sends them. Congregations, as such, may discuss and debate on the issues which are before the church; but they cannot instruct the representatives in the sense that the representatives are controlled. Each congregation sends their pastor and an elder to represent them at presbytery meetings. Synod representation does not represent every congregation normally, and General Assembly representation which is made up of men elected by the presbyteries primarily is based on the total membership of the congregations within the presbyteries. There are some good reasons for believing that our own national government is based upon the Presbyterian system, but whether this be true or not we can understand Presbyterianism by an examination of the civil government or we can understand civil government by observation of the Presbyterian system. They certainly are parallel ways of getting at a government resting on the representation of the people.

The Episcopalian and Congregational Forms of Government

The other two forms of church government are the Episcopalian and the Congregational. The Episcopalian form of government has its center of control in the office of the bishop. Again we follow the moves from the local congregation to certain larger special units (the district, for example, in Methodism), but eventually we reach a bishop who by virtue of his office and such administrative help as he needs rules the church and his bishopric. On occasion, depending on the church using this system of government, the House of Bishops meets and control is centered there.

In the Congregational form of government, if we look at it purely theoretically as opposed to some practices in the system, the church as the church is the congregation. Congregational groups may join together in all kinds of loose federations to accomplish purposes in some geographic area, or they may unite more formally to launch a foreign mission program, for example, or to support a theological seminary. In case of differences, however, that might lead eventually to a showdown, the power resides in the congregation itself. They may seek guidance from some larger group or some other congregation, but they are neither directed by a bishop nor are they under the control of the decisions of any other congregations or groups of congregations. I remember once being approached by a college professor who was concerned about his coming marriage to a divorced woman. He asked me what my personal view on his question might be, and this was about all I could give him, but I suggested that he ought to follow the guidance of his church in such a decision. I was interested to discover that the church in his case meant the local congregation, and since he had no particular trust in his own pastor, he did not know where else to turn. I understand that eventually he sought and followed the advice of a professor in one of our theological seminaries.

Historically the Episcopal form of government in the church allied itself, or more exactly felt more at home, in a monarchial form of civil government. At the time of Cromwell, for example, in the history of England, it was to be expected that the bishops allied themselves with the king. At the other end of the spectrum were the congregations who represented the fiercely individualistic radical movements not only in England but also on the continent. The Presbyterians were at some half-way house. Milton once said, "New presbyter is old priest writ large," because he recognized that the Presbyterians believed in a strong church government, but it was also true in Milton's time that the Presbyterians opposed both bishop and king. Significantly, as we shall point out later, because these forms of church government were so closely allied with forms of civil government, great efforts were made to establish the form of church government under the direction and command of the Scriptures, thus giving Scriptural authority to the civil government.

Although no church government now would too strenuously support its particular form from Scripture proof texts, there was a time in the history of the church when people who held to one or another of these forms of government were sure that they based their own peculiar position on the commands of Scripture. Just recently I came on an interesting illustration of these kinds of serious viewpoints. A book for study classes by G. I. Williamson, a pastor in Auckland, New Zealand, called the *Westminster Confession of Faith* presents the following outline as a kind of proof that the Presbyterian system is the *right* one, and I am sure that his chart and following comments clearly reflect the position of the Westminster divines when the Westminster Confession was drawn up, and surely represent the great confidence with which groups in that day supported their position with Scripture.

The Principles of Scripture	*Hier.* (or Episcopalian)	*Cong.*	*Presb.*
1. Christ alone is head of the church (Eph. 5:23, Col. 1:18, etc.)	No	Yes	Yes
2. Elders are chosen by the people over whom they are to rule (Acts 1:15-26, 6:16)	No	Yes	Yes
3. All ruling officers (elders-bishops) are equal in authority (Acts 20:7, 28, Titus 1:5, 7)	No	Yes	Yes
4. Each particular church must have a plurality of elders (bishops) (Acts 14:23)	No	No	Yes
5. Church officers (elders-bishops) are ordained by the presbytery (i.e., a large body of elders drawn from churches in communion) (I Tim. 4:14)	No	?	Yes
6. The right of appeal from the smaller to the wider assembly of elders (Acts 15:1-31)	No	No	Yes

Observe how Mr. Williamson comments on this chart.

> Inasmuch as the presbyterian form of church government is the *only* form of church government which is agreeable with these biblical principles, truth requires that we testify that it alone is sanctioned by Christ, and that the other forms are without warrant from the Word of God. This does not mean that churches without presbyterian government are necessarily to be declared false churches (nor that all churches that preserve presbyterian government are true churches). But as far as government is concerned no church is pure unless it is presbyterian.

It seems to me that this statement of G. I. Williamson would represent the pure theory of Presbyterianism with its Scriptural foundation reflected in the Westminster Confession of Faith. In matters of practice Presbyterianism has gone far afield from this kind of dogmatism. In the first place, under the pressure of other churches and other forms of government and particularly under the pressure in our day of the ecumenical movement it has been almost impossible for the Presbyterians to hold a positive position even theoretically. Many examples could be brought forward to illustrate this drift. There is, for example, a very large congregation in the Presbyterian church which operates almost on Congregational principles because the pastor and many of his session members are not in harmony with the theological slant of modern Presbyterianism. They are careful to earmark many of their funds for work in other churches which are more closely in harmony with their own theological position. In addition to this, they publish their own Christian education materials and run their own summer camp program. What is true of this one church is more or less true of many churches.

Presbytery is very careful about acting against a church of any size or of considerable wealth if that church wishes to run according to its own rights. In recent years, I have heard it said by some pastors of some churches that whereas they are in agreement with what the denomination as a whole is doing with regard to the New Confession, for example, they think it wise to pay attention to their own flock and their own immediate needs and let the denomination move as it wishes.

We know how easy it is in our civil responsibilities to pass responsibilities on to other people who are politically minded and who "care" about that sort of thing. So it is in the church. Ministers become relatively irresponsible in presbytery matters, and frequently the elder who is sent to Presbytery from a congregation is the one who has time to go to the meeting instead of the one who is most able to participate in presbytery and most able to represent his congregation. It is always easy in a representative form of government to "let George do it," and this points up the other side of the problem. Increasingly what ought to be done responsibly in presbytery is passed on into the hands of those who are willing to take authority and who eventually take over power. This means that frequently the Presbyterian form of government drifts over into an Episcopalian form of government. Although the terminology is different it is always true that a presbytery executive or a synod executive in both action and power is not very far removed from being a bishop and exercising a bishop's control.

In some branches of Presbyterianism power has moved in the direction of board secretaries. In other Presbyterian groups it has moved to the theological seminaries, and in other groups it has moved to the general assembly or the office of the stated clerk. These men who hold high office in the church may not necessarily seek this power or want it, and they may very well exercise themselves carefully trying to force the power back to the presbyteries where it belongs. But by carelessness and indifference the power which ought to reside in the true representation of presbytery tends to drift toward certain power centers. Thus it is that a fine representative form of government, fine, that is, in theory, may move in either the direction of Congregationalism or Episcopalianism.

This sort of thing is observable not only in Presbyterianism but in other forms of church government. In the Methodist church which is an episcopalian form, a bishop is very hesitant to move in authoritatively on the life and policies of a strong and wealthy congregation. At the other end of the spectrum Congregational churches find it increasingly necessary to set up offices and officials which will represent congregations in working out programs on a state-wide or national basis. By the very nature of their denominational program some things have to be done far beyond the bounds of the local congregation; and, therefore, have to be controlled by someone who does not necessarily have a congregational relationship.

We are constantly in the same sort of bind in the states rights versus federal government concepts. We recognize the necessity of democratic or republican reponsibilities, but we also recognize what has to happen when we work as a nation over against other nations in times of war, for example, or when even in internal matters, something bigger than state government is necessary for the control of national parks, rivers and harbors, or water supply. With larger masses of people and increasing complexity of life it is very difficult indeed to protect the democratic or republican principles of either our national or church organizations.

The pressure of time also plays its part. Things have to get done within certain time limits. Monies move into the church coffers which have to be used within a budgetary year, and so decisions have to be made on those levels where they can be made immediately and sometimes arbitrarily. How any church structure can escape this sort of thing in our day is difficult for me to see.

Adolph Harnack, an outstanding German church historian of the past generation, probably one of the greatest experts in the field, was the one who first suggested that "theory follows practice in church government." He looked on any theory of church government as a kind of rationalization. Men recognized first of all that a certain form of government was needed, and then they developed the reasons why such a form of government should be established. We could perhaps understand this by observing the development of a dogma in the Roman Church such as the infallibility of the Pope. It was quite normal in the history of the early church that members of the church should seek advice and guidance on church matters. Paul's first letter to the Corinthians is built entirely around problems which have arisen in the Corinthian church, to which problems he writes with the authority of an apostle. By the time the apostles had passed on, certain strong leaders had arisen in the patristic period, and they tended to be located in large urban centers close to a library or to a university.

Leaders of the church arose in centers such as Jerusalem, Antioch, Alexandria, and especially Rome. It was natural for men to look to Rome for leadership because of centers of power and authority in that locale. It was also normal that in a city like Rome the odds would be in favor of strong, able men rising to positions of authority. If the church wanted information and guidance, where would it naturally turn? So they turned to Antioch or Alexandria, but increasingly to Rome. By the same token men of ability tended to move toward Rome for the same reason that the Apostle Paul had set his mind on preaching eventually in the Eternal City.

What men did by practice or habit meant eventually that the powers given to the leaders in Rome were eventually assumed by that leadership. As the church competed with the Roman state and then with the paganism of the Middle Ages, men of great strength guided the destinies of the Roman Church. Many times they needed power and authority and needed it immediately, and some were not hesitant to assume powers which the church had not yet given to them. The "Forged-Decretals" were a clumsy attempt to justify authority in Rome, but eventually it was possible anyway with the viewpoint that Rome had in tradition as well as in Scripture, for the powers of the Pope to be justified. Thus in the middle of the nineteenth century the "infallibility of the Pope" was established as church doctrine. As Harnack stated, "theory follows practice."

Presbyterianism and Democracy

In Protestantism we can see the same sort of thing taking place. Democratic systems of government can often turn over their rightful authority to those who are willing to put out the effort to use the authority. That the authority is abused is not surprising in either church or state although the Presbyterian system, for example, still maintains the checks and balances by which absolutism or tyranny can be stopped. Nevertheless the changes take place according to the rising needs of the church, and in due time changes in structure are "justified" or "rationalized." Theory follows practice.

Again in Protestantism we have a wide variety of places and situations in which the church is at work. It is all well and good to say that a church should have ministers and elders and presbyteries and synods, but it is perfectly evident that in a primitive situation in a mission field where the total church membership may be no more than a dozen souls there is no place for this kind of ecclesiastical complexity of organization, and certainly to get the job done the missionary or evangelist must exercise authority which does not necessarily rest in the theory of government of his own church. He may hope to move in the direction of that theory, but even so in his case the theory has to follow the practice.

One of the great experiments in the ecumenical movement in our day has been the rise of the Church of South India. This experiment brought together not only the varied liturgies and theologies of several denominations but actually united Episcopal, Presbyterian, and Congregational forms of government. If we can observe that movement after the fact, we can see that the leaders in that area felt that the work could be better done by a single church than by conflicting denominations. The idea of union led to the bringing together of diverse forms of government, and a form of government was then established in order to fit the need. Theory followed practice.

As long ago as John Calvin, who was a practical church statesman as well as a theorist, one can read out of the *Institutes* (although we may be often in danger of reading into them) that Calvin's viewpoint was something like this. The needs of the church dictate the forms of government required to answer those needs. The New Testament church as reflected in the book of Acts and the epistles had similar needs in diverse situations and made provision for those needs. A church now, therefore, is "Biblical" not in following slavishly the dictates of the New Testament; but the church is "Biblical" when, in seeking the organization and officers necessary for the needs of its own day, it taps the Biblical sources instead of inventing or creating offices which are not Biblical. If a church needs a bishop (synod executive, district superintendent, or what you will), there are bishops in the New Testament church. If a church has to operate a single congregation, there are reflections of this sort of thing in the "gathered congregations" of the New Testament. When Paul was simply preaching from "house to house," we may be sure that there was no sophisticated church structure.

The church of our day needs the framework of organization. It answers needs as they arise with a useful organization, and it needs the contol of the Bible record of the New Testament church to keep from running off in all directions and organizing whatever it pleases. Both freedom and control are required for solid church government.

To turn in an entirely different direction, we ought to note that the Westminster divines were much concerned about "the keys of the kingdom of heaven" (see "Of Church Censures," *Westminster Confession of Faith*). In the Roman structure the interpretation of the keys of the kingdom is related to Peter and the popes who presumably followed in his turn. The keys of the kingdom were given to Peter, and the Roman church holds that these keys are passed on to subsequent popes by virtue of their office. This gives to the papacy and to the descending orders of the papal system the right "to bind and loose," in other words, to control a man's eternal destiny by giving or withholding communion. Related to this belief are such heresies, as the Protestant would view them, as the sacrament of penance, the confessional, purgatory, and some of the absolute temporal powers maintained by the Curia.

What does Protestantism do in place of what they condemn in Rome? They hold that there ought to be confession and absolution, but that this confession and its absolution do not rest on any action of the church, but on the assurances or reassurances of the promises of the Scripture. The minister does not absolve in his own name or in the name of the church. He simply reiterates the promises of the Gospel which are available to those who make a true confession.

With regard to "the keys of the kingdom" and the "binding and loosing," it is the Protestant belief that the preaching of the Gospel looses men from sin and the guilt of sin and meanwhile serves as a judgment on those who will not respond to the Gospel. There is a binding and a loosening, but not because of the minister or because of the organization of the church. A. J. Cronin, who had a mixed Catholic-Protestant parentage, wrote a book called *The Keys of the Kingdom*. He himself was a

Roman Catholic, but his interpretation of this phrase in his book is a Protestant interpretation. A faithful Roman Catholic priest in a lonely outpost in China by his sacrificial life and his sure word of the Gospel releases men from the prison house of sin.

Closely related to this is the whole question of excommunication, and here the Protestant church picks up in its own fashion what is also done by the Romanist. In Presbyterian law, and here again we speak more of theory than practice, there is a place for discipline. Most of us have looked into church records of 50 to 100 years ago and been amazed at the way in which elders in the church or presbyters of the presbytery expected not only to guide the flock but also to discipline them. That they seem to us now to have been overly judgmental is beside the point. What they took seriously was that the church in both belief and practice is supposed to be a community of the faithful and that there are those who by faith and practice do not belong in such a community. There is nothing necessarily Pharisaical about this; there is rather consistency. Calvin put it this way. "We do not pass a judgment on the wolf so much as we protect the flock." No group of elders can possibly believe themselves good enough to pass God's judgment on a man, and they can do so only in terms of the congregation which they represent and in terms of the Scriptures toward which they have made their holy vows. They are in the position of judge on the bench. The judge on the bench does not pass a judgment because he wants to tell the world that he is a better man than the criminal. He passes his judgment in terms of something bigger than himself and bigger than the criminal, namely, the law. His only judgment is whether the criminal has broken the law by which law there follow certain penalties.

Not only in the Presbyterian churches but in the practice of all churches of Protestantism, excommunication or even minor disciplines have now virtually disappeared. Our concern ought to be whether these practices have disappeared because we no longer believe they have any validity, or whether they have disappeared by carelessness and finally by default. It is an entirely different thing to change our practices because we have a better view of truth than it is to change our practices because we can no longer "stand" the responsibilities and the difficulties which representative office requires of us. The general condition of most of our denominations now reflects our own willingness to make clear the requirements of church membership and to keep clear the requirements of continued membership in a church. The criticism is pretty well founded that it is easier to join and stay in a church than it is to join and stay in a service group.

What must be clearly kept before us is that church discipline is for the sake of the church, and also for the sake of the offender. The discipline as an act does not end with that act; but can be a means, if properly used, of making clear to the offender what his relationship to Christ entails; and thereby, it is hoped and prayed, bring him to renewal of his Christian faith and practice. "A little leaven leavens the whole lump." And in the long run a church weakened by lack of discipline can destroy in its own witness the very thing it was organized to witness.

The Ecumenical Movement

One of the strongest drives in the life of the church today is the ecumenical movement. Paul raised the question a long time ago, "Is Christ divided?" How could He be? And if the church is the body of Christ, how can it be divided? John Calvin asked his own question in the light of Paul's question. "Christ is divided, who bleeds?" No Christian can rest happily in the divisions of the church, and so there is good reason for the ecumenical concern. At the same time, we must not be blinded to the fact that forms of church government and offices in the church had their original rationale and justification. We can decide now that they are irrelevant and discard them, but only if we take them seriously for they originated in all seriousness. So with the discipline in our churches, everyone could wish that everything in the church is for everybody. The only question is whether such an easy circumstance is true. People must be loved by the church and by the church members but not sentimentally. In the long run there is no real love apart from rectitude.

CHAPTER 9 – *Questions for Discussion*

1. What is the difference between congregational, episcopal, and presbyterian structures in church government?
2. Why is it believed that the presbyterian system and the American system of government are thought to be parallel?
3. Distinguish between a presbytery, synod, and general assembly.
4. What point does G. I. Williamson in his book, *Westminster Confession of Faith,* make regarding the validity of the presbyterian structure?
5. How does one form of church government tend to move over into the other two forms?
6. Explain Harnack's statement, "theory follows practice in church government."
7. Explain "the keys of the kingdom" from the Roman Catholic and the Protestant viewpoints.
8. Do Presbyterians believe in excommunication?
9. Should Presbyterians work toward a single church in the ecumenical movement?

Chapter Ten

RESURRECTION AND THE JUDGMENT

We should recall here what was said in an earlier chapter regarding the nature of man. He is made up of dust of the earth, elemental stuff, inbreathed with the breath of life; and, as the second chapter of Genesis tells us, man became "a living soul." Man as man, therefore, is body and soul. Others may speak of him as flesh and spirit or matter and energy. As long ago as the beginning of the creation story, men were faced with the problem of their own nature, and in many religions and philosophies the dual nature of man was thought of as a conflict as, for example, between the ways of the flesh and the ways of the spirit.

In the history of human thought attempts have been made to resolve this dualism. A religion like the Hindu religion, for example, might look upon the body and indeed all matter as illusion. In a kind of philosophy called idealism everything material is basically idea, someone's idea; and, therefore, there is no problem between spirit and body because all is spirit or idea or some kind of divine energy. Another solution to the dualism is one which is acceptable in many quarters today: the psychology of behaviorism. This resolution of the problem says that everything is finally matter or the body and can be dealt with mechanically. Even our thinking which appears to us as an experience different from a physical experience can be judged by a behaviorist as simply a very complex arrangement of stimuli and responses. Another solution comes under the heading of Gestalt where the division between soul and body is resolved by calling a man a soul-body, a totality which ought not to be or cannot be divided into its components.

The Scriptures are very clear in keeping alive the dualism between soul and body. Even though the soul and body together make a human being, the two entities can be treated separately and have their own nature and their own existence and, therefore, their own destiny. At the same time they can operate as one person.

The Greek thinkers are generally in harmony with this kind of thinking, and popular thinking goes along the same lines. This is why the immortality of the soul has been a belief in many quarters as it was given classic treatment by the Greeks and especially by Plato. There is a soul substance, and one of the characteristics of this soul substance is its immortality. Plato even went so far as to suggest that this immortality runs in two directions; that is, the soul has always existed and the soul always will exist. It is out of this idea that we get the transmigration of souls where every living soul finds its abiding place first in one person and then in another, or to follow the thinking of the Hindus, sometimes in an animal. The soul moves from one body to another. It has never lacked substance, and it will never cease to be.

The idea of the immortality of the soul is not contrary to Christian thinking although we have to keep in mind that in the basic Christian statements, such as the Apostles' Creed, the Christian says plainly that he believes in the resurrection of the *body*. Whatever existence the soul may have of its own it will not finally be a disembodied spirit. It will be what Paul calls "a spiritual body" or "a resurrection body," but we are not to be spirits or ghosts or wraiths. We are to be embodied.

At the same time a peculiar problem arose around this immortality of the soul and the resurrection of the body, and this problem has found its way into the basic statements of many of our denominational creeds and is certainly clearly set forth in the Westminster Confession (XXXI). The problem is this. It is perfectly evident from human experience that when life goes out of a man his body returns to the elements from which it came. If men believe in the resurrection of the body and the body very plainly is in the grave, where at that moment in time is the immortal soul? The answer is given, and it is an answer that was debated strenuously at the time the Protestant creeds were being written, that the souls of believers move immediately into the presence of God where apparently they carry on some undefined and undefinable spiritual existence, whereas the souls of unbelievers move immediately into the torments of hell. This, of course, raises the question as to why there should be a last judgment at all since the judgment has already taken place in the division between heaven and hell. And this, of course, opens up the whole question of the immortality of the soul apart from the body.

Soul Sleep

One of the earliest writings of John Calvin opposed strenuously those who in his day believed in what they called soul sleep, their view being that at death the soul blots out until the judgment day when soul and body together are brought to judgment. Scriptural support for Calvin's position is very sketchy indeed (one example being the story of the rich man and Dives), and the more one thinks about it the more difficult it is to bring such a view into any kind of sharp or assured definition. Perhaps our problem rests in the fact that when we die the future life, which we call eternal life, is a move into an order of existence which is not governed by our experience of time, what is called the eternal order. Our problem then is that we are trying to fit into a timeless or eternal order of reality the necessary time sequences of our earthly life. A simple illustration would come from our own experience of sleep where in a very brief nap time we might have a very long series of experiences or where we might sleep for a very very long time without any conscious experience of time passing at all. I am inclined to believe, although I can't imagine how I could prove this, one way or another, that what has been characterized as a period of soul sleep will be, as far as the person is concerned, an experience of immediacy. The next experience after one's death will be the judgment. This view at least has the virtue of eliminating a double judgment, the first one dividing people between heaven and hell, and the second judgment doing the same thing all over again, because of the "deeds done in the body."

There is another problem which seems to bother people, and that is how we may have the resurrection of the body when so many different things can happen to a body in death. People have been amused for a good many years (in a gruesome sort of way) by a newspaper account some years ago with the heading, "Who Ate Roger Williams' Bones?" A historical society set out to dig up Roger Williams' bones and bury them in a better place only to discover that an apple tree had grown on his original burial plot, and much of Roger Williams had ended up in apples, and the apples had ended up in a lot of other people whose bodies were eventually committed to the earth. What then had happened to the body of Roger Williams, and in how many others bodies had he moved, and where would his body be on the Day of Judgment?

I can think of a sailor losing an arm or a leg to a shark in the South Seas, losing an arm or a leg in an accident on shore leave, and eventually being eaten by cannibals in a mis-adventure on some far off island. What happens to his body on the last great day in the light of what has happened to it already?

This is a good place to remind ourselves about the nature of our bodies as we possess them now. We must keep reminding ourselves that they are *elemental* stuff, and the *elements* which feed us and make our bodies come from a variety of sources. At any given meal we could eat food from five or six parts of the country or even five or six parts of the world. According to the wonder of our natures we are put together by what we eat. It becomes our body and not the body of someone else. In other words, we are "clothed upon" by this body material.

At the same time our body is constantly being sloughed off. Every time we take a bath many cells of our body disappear, and they say that over a period of seven or eight years every cell of the body is replaced so that a man who has lived to the age of thirty-five or forty has already had five complete "bodies." There is a sense in which five bodies have already died to be replaced by the sixth body. But keep clearly in mind that as each body replaces the other, it is *his* nature so that even in the aging process he is recognizable. Strangely enough with this constant flux there is an identity which does not vary. Thus if a man stole something when he was twenty years of age, even with his new body, he feels guilty about the theft at forty years of age. This is the great field for psychoanalysis, the continuity of a person's reality over the shifts and turns of bodily existence. His feelings of guilt at the age of forty may very well affect the mechanism of the body which he then possesses even though the act which gave rise to the sense of guilt occurred years and years before.

What I am driving at is this. All people are being constantly "clothed upon" by a body which is theirs, which is identifiable, and which has a continuity with the living past; and the new thing that is guaranteed in the resurrection as Scripture portrays it, is that we shall be "clothed upon" with a body (described as we said before as a spiritual body or a resurrection body) which will also have this continuity and be identifiable. The chief difficulty in my own thinking is that there is promise in the resurrection that these new bodies will be like the new life, flawless and free in ways that we cannot now even imagine. How my body will be flawless and still recognizable is beyond me!

What the Biblical revelation seems to insist on and what Presbyterians hold to after they have wrestled with the question of soul sleep is that we are to have a future life enough like the life which we now experience that we may enjoy bliss or terror in the same sort of way but in an intensity of which we now have only a suggestion. If we may stay on the side of the positive, the last judgment for those who are saved moves them into an order of existence where there will be identity, remembrance, continuity, and at the same time, freedom from all those ills which afflict us here below.

The Bible and the Future Life

I think it is significant, and a safe guideline for us, that the Bible is very hesitant to describe the future life in any detail. We are, however, given the firmest kinds of assurances, and because we are Christians we rest our resurrection on the Resurrection of Christ and the promises of Christ which surround that fact. Perhaps a good illustration of the necessary hesitancy of the Scriptures to go into detail is in the move which we all naturally make through pre-adolescent to post-adolescent life. To a ten-year old boy who hates girls it is a little difficult to delineate for him the possibilities of a good marriage. It would be possible to describe the whole thing in detail, but it certainly would not be understood by him in any experiences of his life up to that time nor by any analogy or parallel that you might try to use for illustration. At the same time when he has reached the age of twenty and has a new body with new powers and new desires, it will no longer be necessary to argue or to describe the possibilities of his new life because he will then be the possessor of his new life.

We must surely be in something of this same situation this side of the grave in trying to understand the far side of the grave. We are earth bound (and sinful), limited in our intelligence and vocabulary, hemmed in by the necessity of time, and we are trying to describe a new life in which there will at the same time the kind of continuity that there would be between a ten-year-old and a twenty-year-old and yet a kind of discontinuity because we have moved into a new era or into a new order.

It was Kepler, the great astronomer, who said, "The Bible is not written to describe how the heavens go but how to go to heaven." We are faced with something of the same sort of thing here. The thrust and emphases of the Bible are not descriptions of the future life, but assurances of the fact of that future life based on the kind of life which is lived here and now. Over and over again in the Scriptures, it seems to me, the attention of the reader is turned away from speculations on future possibilties to recommendations of present necessity and especially present moral decisions. The exercise of faith is constantly forced into the picture by our willingness to say in effect that in the light of what Scripture does say this is what I am called on to do now, and what is to come to pass rests with God; the same God, may I remind you, who is revealed in a person called Jesus Christ with the love and concern which he constantly exemplifies toward humanity. Christ was not sent to "judge the world, but that the world through him might be saved." Our God who is revealed in Christ apparently thought what lay ahead for humanity was worth the cross. "Eye hath not seen nor hath it entered into the heart of man" what He has in store for His children.

The Judgment

What do Presbyterians believe concerning the judgment? One peculiar emphasis which we have already treated is that salvation is for the elect. In common with other Christians, Roman Catholics, like most Protestants, hold that judgment is based on the acceptance or denial of what God has done for them in Jesus Christ. Christ Himself said that His very presence among men in His own day was a means by which they judged themselves. How did they react to the truth which they saw in Him? Perhaps this is where the judgment really lies. Sin is spoken of most clearly in Scripture as rebellion or enmity. I think Christ was saying to His hearers that judgment would be on them in terms of whether they rebelled against the right which they did see in Him.

Take the story of the rich young ruler, for example, who "came running" to ask Jesus the question which in his best thinking bothers every man. "What must I do to be saved?" When Jesus told him what the block was in his own life, it was perfectly evident to the man that his possessions lay between what he already had and the vision of something better which was why he "came running," but he turned away sorrowfully not because he had not seen the light, but because he rebelled against the light demanded of him. I think it is perfectly clear that he was not as good a man after his decision as he was before his decision. It is one thing not to see the light. It is an entirely different and more serious thing to see the light and then refuse it, to prefer to hold on to the thing which keeps you from following what you know to be the truth.

This is how Christ judges men. It is not really because they do not understand Him and do not understand what He offers. Very plainly they rebel against what this demands of their lives, and I think Christ's judgment affects men at every level of their progress and of their living. He, therefore, has something to say to the child in the faith and the saint far down the road. Even Paul recognized that he did not do the things he ought to do and he did the things he ought not to do, but he was wise enough to throw himself upon the gift of salvation which is the grace which accompanies the judgment. We accept the finished work of Christ because we cannot work out our own salvation. In such a brief treatment as this one cannot analyze this problem at every level, but I think every reader understands it on his own level. As Paul phrases it, "Who shall deliver me from the body of this death?" That is the drag of all those things we want to hang on to (the rich young ruler and his riches) when we know that we ought to follow the light at any cost; and, of course, this is why the cross is the central symbol of Christianity because there is a cost.

This still leaves a moot question. Suppose one has never heard the Word or seen the light? I suppose there is no ques- that comes at me in student groups more often than this. What about the heathen who have never heard the Gospel or have never had a chance to make a Christian decision? There are several answers to this although I am not sure that they are finally satisfactory. In the first place, if the questioner is sincere instead of just trying to carry on an argument in which he hopes to make the Christian religion look ridiculous, then I think we need to say to the sincere questioner something like this: "If you are really concerned about the heathen being lost, you have just received your first call to be a missionary." This is not said facetiously because as we have already suggested we are taking the question and the questioner seriously.

A second line of approach is this: Christians do not say there are not other ways by which a man can be saved. What they do say is that men will not be saved apart from what Christ has done for them. There may be other ways for God to get after men's hearts and enlighten them. One theory of the "last days" is that the Jews will be converted en masse, *as a people,* which has been their unique nature from the beginning. In any case, the spirit of God is not limited by our understanding of His workings. The only thing that is clear to a Christian is that he is under a mandate which is called "the great commission." This mandate is perfectly clear; once again, there is our rebellion, or our prime concern for other things, to keep us from obedience. It is not a question of light or truth, but a question of obedience and commitment.

Presbyterianism and Sin

In the third place, and finally, and this is the one that hurts, we have in general a highly superficial view of sin. One professor of mine called sin insanity. There is a kind of irrational madness about a creature rebelling against his own Creator; or, if you like, a living thing trying to cut himself off from the source of his own life. The only clue we really have to the nature of sin is the cross of Christ. We think of it as a symbol of salvation. It was first of all a symbol of sin. The best government of the ancient world, the Roman government, and the best religion of the ancient world, Judaism, conspired together, even over against their own hatred of one another, to crucify the Lord of life.

What is this condition in the best of men that simply cannot stand absolute goodness? Why do we always try to shave it off, or tear it down, or blot it out? Why do we want to dispatch people who are "good"? Why are we glad to see that others are not as good as they try to make out, as if somehow this could satisfy us? If Jesus had to go to the cross because of men's sin and to cover sin, then sin is much more serious, desperately so, than we like to think of it when we try to call it modern or sophisticated or try to excuse it by suggesting that after all, men are not any better than they need to be. Once in awhile we get hideous exhibits of sin's true nature as when, for example, the most brilliant nation of our day used its brilliance for the experiments of a Dachau. Why is it true in a world where 98 per cent of the people want peace that we constantly have war? We are in our own nation continually justifying ourselves as peace-loving, and we have never had a period of 25 years in our national life where we have not been at war. What is *wrong* with human nature?

Calvinists in the iron core of their theology have always insisted that sin is so bad that nothing more need be said about the justice of God than that all men by their very nature should go to hell. They have insisted that it is a sign of God's grace that He should save anyone at all. According to the nature of sin and according to the nature of the holiness of God how could such a God elect to save even one sinner? From our viewpoint men seem somewhat lovable and savable, and in the large not bad. Whether this is an exhibit of their true nature only Freud and Dachau can suggest to us. As long ago as the writing of the Bible there were such expressions as the "exceeding sinfulness of sin." No philosopher could work it into his system of thought. The classic Greek tragedies even of the pagan world used it as the starting point of the human problem. The classic plot in all literature is one of sin and guilt, and then a nice question, can there be redemption?

Although the Calvinist tradition looks exceedingly harsh as against the grace of God in the choice of only some for salvation, we can only read what is said if we can somehow put ourselves in Calvin's position which is almost impossible to do in our free and easy day. You must allow for unimaginable heinousness in sin. When you put into this utter separation between holiness and sin the willingness of God in Christ to suffer for the salvation of *any* of fallen humanity you at least understand something of the viewpoint of the first reformers.

Most Presbyterians today cannot stomach the "horrible decree" of Calvin. It is still written into Presbyterian creeds, however, and perhaps should not be criticized until we stand where Calvin stood when he was able to make the statements he did. In Presbyterian creeds generally since the day of the Westminster Confession there has been a shading off of judgment, and consequently a shading off of election with an accompanying resurgence of another truth of God; namely, His inescapable love. It is still a nice question, however, how a person can love me without *choosing* or *electing* to do so. When I am the object of someone's love, I feel that I have been chosen (elected if you like); and isn't it an interesting experience in love that if you feel yourself loved you know automatically that you are unworthy, and the higher your thought of the person who loves you the more amazed you are that he should have chosen *you*? It is strange how this runs up and down the scale. If you have a low regard for the person, you have a low regard for his choice of you for friend or loved one. If you have a high regard for the other person, you are increasingly aware of the wonder that he should love you unworthy as you are. This kind of thinking and this kind of language have been marks of the experience of Christians from the time of the Apostle Paul to the present day. It is because we have too small a concept of God's holiness (and His love!) that we take the whole idea of salavtion so superficially and in the long run without gratitude.

Another endless question with regard to the resurrection and judgment has had to do with the timing of such an event. On the basis of one verse in the book of Revelation, which is an obscure book in many ways, there has arisen the idea that somewhere in the scheme of things there will be a millennium. Some hold that Christ will return to usher in this millennium. They are pre-millennium thinkers. Others hold that men under the Spirit of God will eventually bring to pass the good life on this good earth. Christ will then return at the close of the millennium period, and the judgment of men will take place with His coming. These are post-millennium thinkers. Other believers hold what is called an a-millennium view; that is, they accept the language as figurative and do not believe there is sufficient basis in one verse in Revelation for the building of a doctrine. They hold rather that whatever there is to be said about the millennium actually came with the first coming of Christ and that we live in the millennial period now in which much of life gets better and conversely much of life is capable of getting worse, and that Christ will appear for the final judgment when the number of the elect has reached its fulfillment.

Unless one has carefully looked into these matters he is amazed to discover how many different kinds of churches and denominations have had their individual existence and reason for being because of one or another of these views on the timing of the Second Coming. Presbyterians have never taken an official position on any of these views. They have insisted on the fact of the Second Coming of Christ and on the final judgment based on Him and His work and teaching, but they have never entered into any calendar of events leading up to this fulfillment. Presbyterians hold that it is not given to us to know "the times nor the seasons," but that it is given to us to witness concerning the Gospel until God in His time brings these final things to pass. There is no "Presbyterian" view concerning the millennium.

What can be said for sure concerning the Second Coming is said in a very suggestive phrase: "Those that love his appearing." It is a good test on a man's life whether Christ's return to this earth would make him happy or serve as a grand interference with his plans. What plans and hopes does a man have where the coming of Christ could be an interference?

CHAPTER 10 – *Questions for Discussion*

1. Is a man body or spirit or both? Explain.
2. Do Christians believe in the immortality of the soul or the resurrection of the body?
3. Does the nature of man help to explain the resurrection of the body?
4. How does growth from childhood to maturity help us to understand the resurrection of the body?

5. Why is the Bible hesitant to describe the exact nature of the future life?
6. Are Christians judged now or do they wait the final judgment or both?
7. On what one thing will final judgment be based?
8. Can the heathen be saved apart from Christ?
9. What can be said about the millennium and the end of the world? What do Presbyterians say?

Chapter Eleven

SOCIAL ACTION

One of the strangest facts about Calvinism and its descent through the Reformed tradition is that where it is most Calvinistic, that is, where it is truest to its emphasis on the absolute sovereignty of God, there it most surely releases the free energies of man. Those branches of Protestantism which hold most faithfully to election and predestination strangely enough produce men who seem to be released and free for great accomplishments. This is just the opposite of what one would normally expect. Parallels are often drawn between extreme Calvinism and the Kismet of Islam where the absolute sovereignty of God seems to be interpreted in terms of absolute fate. Everything is so fixed by the action of God that man can excuse himself for what he does and society can be excused for its condition by simply saying, "It is the will of Allah," or "It is Kismet." Men and cultures are paralyzed by fate.

This on the surface is what is the usual criticism of Calvinism. If one believes in the absolute sovereignty of God, if he believes seriously that God initiates and sustains everything that comes to pass and has done so by immutable decrees for all eternity, then it must logically follow that there is nothing for man to do. His course in life is fixed either in his own life or in its complex relationships to society. As a matter of historical fact, however, in those branches of Protestantism where men have most surely held to the absolute sovereignty of God and its concomitant beliefs in predestination and election, we find men working with high commitment and sacrifice to discipline their own lives and thereby change society around them. Why is this so?

Calvin's motto was "Soli Deo Gloria," (To God alone be glory) and his symbol was a hand offering a flaming heart. These two things, motto and symbol, certainly characterized Calvin's life and carried over into the Reformed tradition. Perhaps we understand the Calvinistic emphasis on the sovereignty of God best if we understand that at all costs the glory of God must be maintained. However we may interpret man's rights or freedoms or hopes, these are as nothing over against the glory of God. Thus it was possible for a Puritan divine to say on one occasion that he would be willing to go to hell for the glory of God. If we argue against the absolute sovereignty of God or against predestination or election, the pure Calvinist will answer that even a man's suffering eternally in hell for his sin is, if rightly considered, to God's glory for it establishes God's holiness and justice. It is concern for the glory of God which leads to emphasis on the sovereignty of God. This in turn has its logical conclusion in predestination and election. One might want to fault a religion which is so logical, but because it is so logical, then, once the glory of God forces into a man's thinking the absolute sovereignty of God, one cannot fault the logic.

The Place of God in Calvinism

If to the motto, "To God alone be the glory," is added the picture of the hand offering the heart, we have another clue to the nature of Calvinism. What is man's task here on earth except to give his burning heart to God; and if he be burned up or burned out in the process, what is man as over against the glory of God? We do not think in these ways today for humanism has had its impact, but we do not understand Calvinism unless we can get into that kind of thinking: God first by all, and then we can see what is possible for lost man. However attractive man may be, he is really nothing in terms of the utter glory of God. This hurts our pride, but then as Calvin would insist, pride is the deadliest of the deadly sins and has no place in our discussion anyway. As Isaiah would say it, Even "our righteousness is as filthy rags."

In the Shorter Catechism, which grew out of the Westminster Confession, the first question is, "What is man's chief end?" Then the first answer: "To glorify God and enjoy him forever." How one can enjoy glorifying God in the way the strong Calvinist seems to interpret it is a little difficult for us to grasp, but again the logic is consistent. If everything is of God and unto God, then it would be impossible to enjoy anything outside of God. Our enjoyments apart from God would have us running on the wrong track and eventually running into our own destruction. The trick that led our first parents into sin and, therefore, into destruction, was their belief that they could be "as gods knowing good from evil" and run the whole show on their own terms. Any Calvinist could have told them at the outset that such a thing is absolute folly, and certainly without joy.

This still leads us to the question as to why or how believers in the Calvinistic tradition are so activist in political, social, and cultural affairs. Well, we must start with the heart offered to God. The life is fully given and is given over for the highest possible use. Insofar as a man is capable of succeeding at all his success is measured only to the extent to which he returns to God the life which God has given him. Only this can be his joy and felicity.

Assuming then as the Calvinist must, that our "times are in His hands," we have a special insight into what a Calvinist means by his calling, his sense of vocation. He finds himself "called of God" in the very place where he finds himself and in the task to which he finds himself now given. He can be a doctor or a lawyer or a merchant chief, the point is that he has not arrived at this station in life apart from the will of God for his life. Therefore, in his vocation, whatever his vocation is, he has his "calling," and he is called of God to respond with a heart burning and offered to God. Basically he does not do his task for money or for his own glory, certainly not for success as men would measure success, but all for the glory of God. This puts a special kind of sanctity on a man's job. Luther was talking about this sort of thing when he said that a man could be hoeing nettles or a woman could be rocking a cradle and "such tasks" could be "holy ones."

One of the promises of Scripture is, "Behold I make all things new," and for the Calvinist, "all things" includes *all* things. Therefore, in his task, in his home, and in his citizenship there is supposed to be a total devotion of life to God. And whatsoever his hand findeth to do, he doeth with all his might. This devotion to the task at hand is a calling of God built into a man's daily walk; it releases a new force. He doesn't have to win or he doesn't have to lose in man's terms, but he does have be found faithful; from such a calling there is no escape, "There is no discharge from that war." As Milton puts it, "We walk ever in the taskmaster's eye."

That this seems an overly severe viewpoint regarding a man's daily walk, one can hardly deny. Nevertheless, there is another side. Perry, in his book, *Puritanism and Democracy,* has a chapter which he has titled "The Christian Athlete." He helps us to get inside the thinking of a Calvinist, especially a Puritan. Some of us perhaps had the thrill of seeing the finish of some of the races in the last Olympic Games. At the finish of these races, especially the distance races, there was on the face of the victor a picture of struggle, the giving of his life to the utmost, and yet in the same instant of victory there was a look of grand fulfillment. We speak of "the loneliness of the long distance runner." And surely distance runners know the long thoughts of the daily grind. What does a man think about who, as some of the distance runners do, runs 100 miles in a week or twenty miles in a day? What keeps such a man going? What sustains him? Only that hope of marvelous fulfillment at the moment of victory. Perry says that the Puritan got the same "kick" out of his victories of the spirit as he disciplined his life day after day and as he held to the glorious call to victory as a great athlete gets by his own kind of attainments.

There is a narrow way into life and this, the Gospel assures us, is the truth; but the Calvinist never lost track of the other reality; namely, that whereas the way is *narrow,* the promise is that the life shall be *abundant*. We can see this in all the arts and all the sports. We need to see it in every facet of life. Those of our friends who reach great fulfillment have arrived there by the narrow way and have discovered their self-giving and their self-sacrifice to be justified in terms of the goal. The disciplined life is the only life worthwhile; and, as the Calvinist would reason, why shouldn't this be? The only possible clue to reality finally is the glory of God, and our chief end "is to glorify him." Only thus can we enjoy Him. In our easy-going day, this may be looked upon as hard and even harsh doctrine, but in the long run the truth of it sustains itself as it tests out in individual lives and proves itself over and over again in the stability and integrity of nations. Absence of this spirit in a man or a nation is the first mark of disintegration and decay.

A high sense of duty and a high sense of destiny, therefore, puts a Calvinist into rigorous training, and he is not a real Calvinist unless he rejoices in that very fact. But there is another interesting truth. Picking up the verse, "Make your calling and election sure," the Calvinist, because he believed in election, worried over whether he was really one of the elect. How could one make his calling and election "sure"? Well, the proof had to be seen in results. Calvinists have been criticized for this kind of thinking, but this is the way they did think: If a man is called of God, and if his calling is devoted to God, in some way then the success of his calling ought to give him some assurances.

There is a very tricky business here, however, because if you read this kind of thinking backwards, you come to the interesting conclusion that one may check on his election in terms of his success. And yet in some way, and this is what has always worried the Calvinist, it would be part of his expectancy and of his faith that somewhere, somehow there should be signs of God's seal of approval. We know, of course, that Christ in His calling ended up on a cross, and Paul in his calling ended up in a dungeon and probably on the block, and highly committed Christians in every generation have found no pay-off in terms of worldly success. Here there seems to be some weakness in the logic of Calvinism. Critics of Calvin have been quick to pounce upon this flaw, as a whole library of literature would illustrate.

Calvinism and the Capitalist System

About a century ago, Max Weber wrote an extended essay entitled *The Protestant Ethic and the Spirit of Capitalism.* The essay had a tremendous effect in both sociology and religion, and has been debated pro and con all these years. What is of interest to us here is the kind of case Weber made as illustration of what we have been saying. He laid his emphasis on the expectancy of a good Calvinist that his calling and election would be made sure by the success of his enterprise, and he laid his emphasis also on what we have now come to call the gospel of hard work; namely, that disciplined, continuous effort at a man's task, a task offered to God, can be thought about as a religious exercise. Weber then pointed out that, statistically at least, one could expect that most people getting up early in the morning, working hard all day, being honest as the day is long, and refusing to waste their substance on worldly pursuits would in the long run attain some kind of worldly success.

At the same time as this vocational drive became of religious significance to men, Calvin released the Protestant Church from one of the binding requirements of medievalism by allowing the taking of interest for money invested in productive enterprises. This permission of interest-taking came at the same time that many merchants were expanding their "field of operations" out to the far corners of the earth with the new discoveries of the fifteenth and sixteenth centuries. Men engaged in voyages to the far corners of the earth making long-range investments in money, and those who were interested in investing in that kind of enterprise now had the right to expect some payment for the use of their money. In the large, therefore, this meant that people who worked hard and made money and did not squander their money, had money for investment which in turn made them more money. Coupled with this was their refusal to waste even this new money made out of investment and so it was invested again always with the expectancy of return. What Weber was talking about when he used the phrase, "the spirit of Capitalism," is this combined attitude toward hard work, sound investment, the constant increase of gain, and the refusal as a proper Bostonian would insist later, in ever spending one's principal. As this "spirit of capitalism" became ingrained in the thinking of men, supported as it was originally with some Protestant religious devotion, the whole attitude toward work and money changed from the medieval outlook. In time, however, the "spirit of Capitalism" became divorced from its original religious support and also from its original religious controls, and it was possible in this new "spirit" to believe in work for work's sake (not for the glory of God), and to believe in money for money's sake (and not for the glory of God). Whether this thesis of Weber's will stand up only the debates of the last century can tell, but we have here a wonderful illustration of how what started out as a concern for the glory of God and an acceptance of God's absolute sovereignty along with predestination and election eventuated in sociological attitude and, indeed, some kind of a justification for that attitude. We do not argue the merits of this thesis or even the merits of what happened. We have been concerned to illustrate one way that Calvinism, which might have started out as a kind of fate because everything is of God, ended up with a great many men strenuously working to change things.

Alongside of capitalism and the wider issues of economics, it is interesting to look at what happened in terms of government. This may be observed both in Scotland and England. In Scotland it was perfectly evident to all Protestants that what was basically wrong with Roman Catholicism was the doctrine of works – salvation. This took away from the absolute sovereignty of God by giving some glory to man. The only answer to this was the answer of the Scotch Presbyterians, and the only way he could be sure that God's glory could be manifested in the totality of life was to take firm steps to remove any government which represented any religion so contrary to the glory of God. We must constantly remind ourselves that men did not discuss these matters academically. They really believed them. Rome was not only mistaken but wicked. Protestantism was not only right, but part of the calling of the Calvinist was to put things right for the glory of God. As we have suggested previously, Christians are called to obedience: "The powers that be are ordained of God." But another factor was plainly there. The powers in control were surely not ordained of God because they were so contrary to the clear truth of the Gospel. To the glory of God, therefore, they must be removed and revolution was therefore justified.

In England there was something of the same move climaxed finally in the beheading of Charles the First and the rule of the Protector. This was the right kind of lordship, not a king but a protector, in some sense a shepherd of the flock called not so much to rule as to guide the people of God. That Cromwell became a tyrant and an absolute monarch in his own way was simply the fulfillment of a logic which he himself had not expected. It was so clear to him and his followers that what they did was for God's sake that they eventually were maneuvered into a position of believing that anyone who opposed their rule opposed the rule of God. This is a trap into which many revolutionists have fallen. The difficulty about any revolution is to get the revolution stopped. There is no such thing as a "power vacuum" so that when any one ruling power is removed another power must take over. One of the first requirements of those who rule is that they must rule and, therefore, they must immediately crush any revolutionary elements arising in their own domain.

At the same time, England was plagued (if you like) by a great many independent sects, many of which were marked by a quivering expectancy of the immediate Second Coming of Christ. They believed that God would break in and rule "in England's fair and pleasant land." Others who were equally committed to the Christian faith believed in the immediate rule of Christ apart from His Second Coming. One of the expectancies of their calling in politics was, therefore, that the things of Christ should be brought to bear completely on the affairs of men. We might not agree with their starting places or their viewpoint, but we cannot argue against their consistency. The glory of God has to do with the total life of the total man. The flaming heart was offered, the whole life was committed. This is what a man's calling is all about. This is his vocation.

In terms of the rule of Christ on this earth, therefore, governments must be established on the basis of Holy Writ, and those who oppose this sort of thing are opposing the very Word of God. The pressure of the sects was that their expectancy of the coming of Christ had to be answered by the organization of a government which should bring about the rule of Christ whether Christ returned in the flesh or not. This is superficial treatment, of course. But we see, nevertheless, that a kind of Calvinism which believed in the glory of God and the absolute sovereignty of God was desperately active in glorifying God by changing governments as well as changing men.

It is not necessary to go into sociological schemes. Our illustration would follow the same lines. In due time something had to be done about the awful conditions of labor with the coming of the Industrial Revolution. Something had to be done about child labor, the labor of women, the conditions of slavery and the like. In the city of Geneva in the sixteenth century Calvin moved to clean up the immorality of the bath houses – one might think of this as a moral or religious concern – but he also made his move for the solution of unemployment by the establishment of industry and in the founding of a university which had its effect on education through all of Europe.

Some have argued that this was not the affair of the church and that what Calvin did he did by way of the rulers of the city. We must remind ourselves, however, that the rulers of the city were themselves complete Calvinists and recognized clearly that as Christian citizens they were called upon to change the economy and the social practices of their city. There is considerable debate in our day as to whether the church as a church should act in the area of politics or social improvement, and Calvin in his practices in Geneva is often brought forward as proof text.

I am not sure that the parallel between our times and his is a good one. Two things marked the city of Geneva which are not characteristic of our own time: (1) The separation between the church and the state which we know now did not characterize medieval life and was not clearly in the thinking of Protestantism in Geneva; and (2) people who disagreed with Calvin left town, and people who agreed with Calvin moved into town making Geneva what Knox called "the most perfect school of Christ." In that way it became a peculiar city, almost a theocracy. We could not discover such a community anywhere today unless it should be one of the small pietistic communal groups which are ineffective in our total society. What we can and must learn from Calvin's Geneva is that it was the assumption of the city dominated by Calvinistic religion that sound religion had as a necessary parallel the call to change, not only individual lives and political structures, but also moral and social practices; and in a sense they assumed that bad housing and unemployment called them into action as much as the immoralities of the bath houses.

In any case from that day to this in Scotland and in England, in Holland and in the simple structures of the early colonies in New England, the Calvinistic tradition has never been free of social conscience; and, as we have tried to show in this chapter, this social conscience is most likely to grow up in that soil which is most truly Calvinistic, that is prime concern for the glory of God, the sovereignty of God, a man's calling to God's glory.

Presbyterians and Social Action Today

Presbyterianism in our day is now having its own special debate regarding social problems. There is debate, first of all, as to what is most pressing, whether war, poverty, race, or what. There are those who believe that the prime duty of a church is to preach the Gospel and to save souls, and one cannot fault this as a first concern. The church clearly has a Gospel to preach. But Calvinism in its history would certainly prove that social gains must be worked out primarily by those who are under the urgency of their duty to God.

It has been interesting to observe that in the foreign mission program where the work of the church can be seen more clearly because the structures are frequently more primitive and, therefore, more simple, the evangelistic program of the church expanded into education and medicine, the feeding of the hungry, and attempts to create means of employment or income. It is not at all unusual for a mission compound to include in its activities agriculture, medicine, and education, as well as evangelism.

The home church has not been averse to entering into the lists against drunkenness or prostitution. Where the debate came was when the church began to enter into the lists against racial injustice or bad housing or poverty. Intemperance has been looked upon as a moral issue, bad housing as an economic issue. Presbyterians generally now draw no such lines. As William Temple once said, "All our problems are theological ones." What a man thinks about God and his relationship to God is a theological question which must eventually determine the whole of his life. So with the church in politics or sociology. Religion is for the whole man and churches are made up of such men. In terms of the wholeness of life can one call prostitution a moral problem and then say that bad housing or poverty are not moral problems especially since they are definitely related to prostitution?

There will be in the future other social, economic, and political problems which we cannot now foresee; and so we cannot say ahead of time what the church's attitude should be. It seems clear, however, that in the Presbyterian tradition the church by the very nature of its theology is of necessity called to social action.

CHAPTER 11 – *Questions for Discussion*

1. Explain how Presbyterians can hold to the absolute power of God in all things and still be free for social action.
2. How does Calvin's personal motto help us to understand this?
3. What is meant by the word "vocation" in the Presbyterian tradition?
4. How far out should a man's vocation exercise itself beyond his personal needs?
5. Is God's absolute demand in our life a binding or a releasing reality?
6. Is freedom possible apart from law?
7. What is Weber's contribution to an understanding of Calvinism?
8. If a Presbyterian is "called" to do the will of God in the whole of life, can he possibly escape social action?
9. What does history teach us about the necessity for the church to take a stand in politics and economics?
10. How does the foreign mission program of the church illustrate the place of Christianity in social action?

Addenda

THE CONFESSION OF 1967

As this chapter is being written (June, 1966), "The Confession of 1967" has already been approved and sent to the presbyteries for action according to the action of the General Assembly in May of 1966. Something needs to be said, however, about the form of the Confession as it goes to the presbyteries.

A Committee of Fifteen was appointed by Moderator Thompson for the purpose of revising the Confession as it came from the committee chaired by Dr. Dowey. This committee was chosen to represent a cross-section of the church and included both ministers and laymen and some highly trained theologians. It was not only representative of various theological positions ranging from the liberal to the conservative but was also chosen to represent the church geographically. The purpose of this committee was to revise the Confession as presented by the Dowey Committee in order that the revision might be presented to the General Assembly in Boston in May of 1966. The chairman of this committee of revision was Dr. Sherman Skinner of St. Louis, and under his leadership the work of revision was done with great care and sensitivity. The suggestions for revision came from hundreds of sources including individuals, churches, sessions, presbytery committees and some *ad hoc* groups organized to study the Confession. One of the outstanding groups that came into being for the purpose of studying the Confession was called Presbyterians United for Biblical Confession. They worked over the proposed confession with meticulous care, and sent in a total revision. All these materials were studied at great length in a long series of meetings of Dr. Skinner's committee.

When the General Assembly met in Boston in May of 1966, there were three possibilities for action. (1) The Confession of 1967 could be sent to the presbyteries for vote without revisions i.e. as it was written by the Dowey Committee; (2) the General Assembly could send the revised treatment of the Confession of 1967 as that revision was presented by the Skinner Committee; and, at the same time, the floor of the Assembly was thrown open for further revision, the General Assembly working at the time as a kind of committee as a whole; (3) the General Assembly could reject the Confession of 1967 and refuse to send it to the presbyteries for vote.

The discussion of the General Assembly was marked by great openness for discussion and great care that everyone should be heard and that serious consideration should be given to every possible revision. With some very small changes, however, the revision as presented by the Skinner Committee carried the Assembly and this revised treatment of the Confession of 1967 is now before the United Presbyterian Church for a vote by the presbyteries. It is generally conceded that the presbyteries will vote favorably; and, if so, the Confession of 1967 will be voted on finally by the General Assembly in 1967 and thus become the confessional position of the church.

One of the most interesting developments in the creation of this new confession has been its relationship to what the Dowey Committee referred to as the Book of Confessions. The United Presbyterian Church comes out of the Reformed and Calvinistic traditions and roots back into the great confessional findings in the whole history of the church. The church from its very inception has been making creedal and confessional statements, and those which were determined closest to the Reformed tradition and those most catholic in their temperament were brought together in the Book of Confessions as representative of the confessional position of the United Presbyterian Church. Such catholic statements as the Nicene Creed were brought together with such Reformed statements as the Second Helvetic Confession and the Scots Confession. As understood by the Assembly, the new confession becomes, therefore, the most recent and most contemporary effort on the part of the church in a long doctrinal history in which many such efforts have been made.

It was not clarified in the Assembly, and there is still some debate on the question, as to the relationship to the Book of Confessions. Where there is a difference, which statement should prevail? Frequently when questions were raised about the new confession, the answer was given that the question was already answered in the Book of Confessions. At the same time it was pointed out that the Book of Confessions does not speak with one voice at every point, and that the new confession shows some changes in specifics and some change in spirit from the former confessions. The question is: where the new confession does not speak to an issue is the Book of Confessions then authoritative, and furthermore where there is a difference between the new confession and one of the ancient confessions to what extent is the new confession authoritative? How this question will be resolved is still an open debate in the United Presbyterian Church.

General enthusiasm is reflected over the pertinence of this new confession on the subject of reconciliation. Here the new confession is highly relevant to the needs of our day. Critics today have pointed out, however, that the evidence of reconciliation between man and man needs emphasis on the idea of reconciliation between man and God. The social reconciliation is stated in a masterly way. The saving reconciliation is muted.

There are still those within the Presbyterian Church who are uneasy about the ambiguity regarding universalism and what seems to be something of a departure in the doctrine of Scripture of the Westminster Confession. The Christology is clear and strong regarding Christ's humanity but not so much so regarding His deity.

The social problems of war, poverty, and race are met head on and other social problems are indicated, particularly the questions related to the "new morality." But two questions remain. (1) Would the relevance of this new confession disappear with the solutions of these problems? In other words, is this confession's attempt at relevance possibly only a tract for the times? (2) Is it possible in meeting certain social problems to leave out others; and, if so, would the confession be better as a statement of general principles rather than a specific listing of the social problems of our own particular day?

The Confession of 1967 is of major importance to the life of the United Presbyterian Church in the United States of America. It is of great importance, also, in Protestantism for it may well set the pace for review in other denominations. It is of great importance in the ecumenical movement because it will determine rapprochement possible with other traditions and especially with Rome. From the standpoint of church history it is a tremendously significant document.